Contents

Foreword

Ariel Hyatt is a tireless champion for independent musicians. For the last 22 years I've watched her work in public and behind the scenes. We had many of the same clients, and they all raved about her. She's been on the front lines, working directly with musicians and the media outlets every day. She's very hands-on. She's the real deal, through and through.

I'm thrilled that she's written *The Ultimate Guide to Music Publicity*, to teach you everything she's learned so that you can do it yourself or decide not to.This book is so needed because it's such a misunderstood and counter-intuitive field. It's hard to imagine what it's like to be on the receiving end of your music. She explains the mindset better than I've ever seen, but most importantly gives you concrete action steps so you can begin right away and start getting results.

- Derek Sivers, founder, CD Baby

Dedication

To my son, Aiden.
You are the light of my life.

Introduction

I started working in publicity as an intern between my freshman and sophomore year of college. I was 19 and I had always dreamt of living in London. Luckily for me, I had a family friend who worked in the fashion PR business and he offered me an unpaid internship at his NYC agency's sister firm, Lynne Franks Limited — the hottest PR firm in London at the time. Years later, Lynne Franks Limited became the firm AB FAB, the British TV farce, was based upon. If you've seen that show you probably know where this is going.

I took all of my babysitting and telemarketing money that I had earned in high school and bought a ticket to London. I rented a room in the attic of a sprawling house owned by a quirky family in central London. The bathtub leaked, I had a lumpy futon bed, and my fridge was the size of a shoebox.

I showed up bright-eyed and bushy-tailed on the first day of my internship and upon meeting my supervisor, I asked the question, "So, what exactly is PR?"

I genuinely didn't know the answer to this question. In my defense this was pre-internet 1991, so it wasn't like I could simply Google it. I'll never forget the horrified look on his face.

"PR? It's PR!" was his answer:

I thought, "Wow. Thank you for that."

That internship was a disaster from the get go. Starting that day, I learned that PR was mostly manual labor. I spent every moment putting together packages for members of the media who got an endless supply of free stuff — sneakers, underwear, makeup, all thoughtfully and beautifully packaged up and then delivered by hand courier all across London.

Here's an interview I found from Lynne Franks in PR Week:

> *"PR involved endless phone calls, faxes, and stuffing envelopes with press kits or fancy invitations... We didn't use emails; it was fax, fax, fax. It was insane, because you'd be sending 12 faxes to the same office to different journalists." she recalls."*

> *When we ran events such as London Fashion Week...we'd have a team of couriers waiting. We'd put [printed invitations] into envelopes and then they'd steam them off around to the hotels and journalists' offices. It was all manual labour." - Lynne Franks*

Until I started working in PR firms, I really didn't understand the depth of how PR touches almost everything you read in the media. For example, when you open a magazine and you see "Our favorite shampoo of the year," or "The best pants to wear this season," that is all the work of a publicist. The editor did not go walking around to find the best anything. The publicist worked very, very hard to gain the attention of the editor to place the "best" products, styles, and of course, music that you discover.

My internship lasted five weeks. After being treated like total garbage and feeling totally humiliated by the staff who didn't like the American girl they assumed was in London to spend "Daddy's money," I had to quit. I had never quit anything in my life and at the time it was the biggest defeat I'd experienced. It was that experience (and a few others later in the music business) that to this day feeds my desire to help educate others about the industry.

I did learn a crucial lesson from my first five weeks immersed in PR: If you want to get the attention of the media, the devil is in the details. The thoughtfully prepared package with the perfect bag, ribbon, envelope, and note of yesteryear is equivalent to the perfect email pitch today.

It is my deepest desire to teach you what PR actually is and help you secure some, or hire someone to help. Preferably someone who is kind and compassionate and loves your music.

Ariel

I'm psyched you are here. Whether you're a new artist looking to take your first steps towards getting publicity or a veteran seeking new tips, there is something here for you. The information contained herein comes from my experience working on countless music PR campaigns and from coaching artists through the choppy waters of publicity in the ever-changing music business. Many music industry PR veterans and music journalists, bloggers, and playlist curators have been generous enough to weigh in with their advice and observations.

Music publicity has changed radically over the years from the traditional publicist to journalist model, to a model that now allows anyone with social media access to almost any member of the media.

With COVID-19, artists are now facing new challenges due to a lack of touring and live performance opportunities. Coupled with the hard fact that many newsrooms and outlets have shuttered as a result of the pandemic, the publicity landscape continues to transform.

Here's a harrowing statistic to keep in mind: 60,000 new tracks are released on Spotify every single day.

Here's another one: According to Muck Rack, there are six PR pros to every one journalist.

In short, whether you want to hire a publicist or do it yourself, there's a lot of competition.

Once a music blog or playlist begins to gain traction and solid social media numbers, hundreds of publicists, labels, managers, and artists all start vying for inclusion. In order to stand out from the masses you have to have an understanding of how to communicate effectively, and you must also have a strategy.

Music blogs and playlists frequently come and go. The reason for this is they are mostly created and run by fans who love music and are driven by passion. Sadly, passion doesn't pay the bills and, over time, their enthusiasm wanes and the blogs and playlists shut down.

This means, as an artist, you must consistently cultivate new relationships with outlets as you release new music.This guide will act as a template for how to do this whether you choose the DIY route or hire a professional publicist to help you.

PART 1
It All Starts with Your Brand

1
Music Publicity Today

You probably want publicity because you would like to gain new listeners and fans. You may also be looking for name recognition and notoriety. Or, perhaps you are deeply curious about what music media and tastemakers will say about your music. And it may be possible that you think that if you get enough publicity, bigger and better things will happen to you from a music career perspective.

All of these reasons are valid and absolutely the right thinking. However, after 25 years of launching and executing publicity campaigns, I've learned a lot about the mindset of many musicians and their false perceptions about what publicity does (and doesn't do) for you.

THE OLD MUSIC BUSINESS PARADIGM

Once upon a time, when a musician or band completed an album, the standard industry advice they would get was to immediately hire a publicist. This publicist was pretty much the only way that an artist could gain access to the media. She was retained for a minimum of three months and tasked with writing a long bio that read like a resume filled with every single historical moment in the band's history and all of their achievements and accolades. Next, a photo shoot was arranged and one photo was chosen for the entire press campaign. Then, an official press release was written heralding the arrival of the album. Three months in advance of the album's drop date, this press release (as well as physical packages) were sent to thousands of music journalists and media outlets including newspapers (daily, weekly, and specialty), glossy magazines, TV, and radio. A lot of envelope stuffing would ensue.

The publicist then spent months securing long-lead press (magazines and monthly publications) first, then working her way to the media who operated on shorter deadlines. By the day the album was released, all of the media was secured as the release day was the last possible day for coverage, unless there was a tour booked and then the envelope stuffing and press release blasting process was repeated in each tour market.

A great placement in a substantial newspaper often correlated with sales at record stores in that market and the ultimate - a late night TV slot of a show like Letterman - could turn into a massive spike in sales.

THE NEW MUSIC BUSINESS PARADIGM

Things have changed dramatically.

Today, we live in a singles-based market and in many cases the music is recorded, mixed, and mastered days before it is released online. Long-lead press does still exist but the norm is the media shows up hours or a few days after the pitch goes out.

The evolution of devices, expanding social channels, the 24-hour news cycle, and instant access to every imaginable type of media for all, has shifted the publicity landscape. Media outlets are under enormous pressure to publish content that drives eyeballs and traffic and gets clicks. This is how they survive. Sadly, this means unless you can bring traffic or something truly newsworthy or clickable to the table, the larger outlets will pass you by until you are in a position to help them. Publicity is now a two-way street.

One thing that has not changed is that many artists still believe, and are advised OR and are told that the first thing they should do is hire a publicist. But this should not be the first thing you do. I advise that you start by focusing on your brand and online voice and at least get a few fans before you even think about publicity.

The media no longer trusts only the publicist when deciding on features. With a few clicks they can now easily see the artist's brand, follower numbers, images, back catalog, and videos.

PUBLICITY IS A LONG GAME

It's perfectly ok to have a big fat goal of coverage from a notable newspaper or a national publication. However, if you are just starting with publicity, I implore you to check your expectations at the door.

Starting small and building is the best way to ease into publicity. So, in the beginning, shoot for smaller outlets. There will be plenty of time to build as you go.

Also, the good news is that the day your music drops is, in many ways, the beginning of your publicity journey with hundreds, if not thousands, of online outlets, blogs, podcasts, and playlists to choose from. However, you must also work fast so that your release doesn't get too stale. So, planning is key.

Publicists, of course, can still be invaluable. Nowadays, they work faster, and create shorter bios and even shorter pitches for media who have to cover ten times the amount of music and whose attention is harder than ever to grab.

PUBLICITY DOES NOT SELL MUSIC

If you want publicity or you are hiring a music publicist to see a spike in sales, I have news for you: there is absolutely no correlation between getting publicity and selling music.

Publicity is designed to raise awareness of you in the press, to help build and share your story, and create critical acclaim. Sadly, publicity does not help sales spike as it did in the old paradigm. Of course, a well-placed feature may lead to sales, but overall, if selling music is your goal, publicity should not be the first domain you try to conquer. Why? Because streaming.

For many reasons, people no longer buy music when they love it. The two most predominant are: consumer behavior has changed and music for many is considered free. Also, people already pay for their Spotify, Apple Music, or Pandora subscriptions, (or they listen via free versions). This defines their perception of value - they can literally get all of the music in the world for $9.99 per month.

2
The Musician's Communication Map

There is so much more to music publicity today than simply communication between you and the tastemakers who may grant you exposure — music journalists, blogs, podcasts, TV, radio, and playlisters.

Writing this guide got me thinking about all of the forms of communication that musicians must know how to navigate which also fall under the category of "PR."

Public Relations, or PR, is all of the communications that take place between you and the public as the map will illustrate.

Music publicists are professionals who help musicians by securing various unpaid or earned communications. In the new music business it's not always unpaid. There's a grey area here, as well as fee-based submissions, which I will break down in this guide.

A music publicist can help with traditional media, social media, and securing in-person events like award show invitations, or red carpet events.

Publicity is simply attention given to someone or something by the media.

Many people confuse PR with publicity but there is a huge distinction.

I felt the need to share these with you so you could expand upon any narrow definitions you may have of publicity because as you can see, almost every time you turn to your smartphone or computer to communicate, some form of it is at hand.

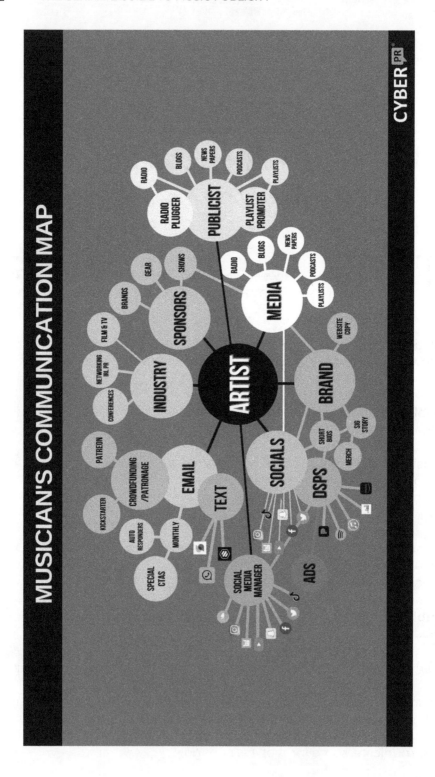

I created The Musician's Communication Map so that you could have a visual representation of all of the domains where a solid communication strategy is necessary. As you can see, this includes traditional media, social media, and in-person engagements.

THE MUSICIAN'S COMMUNICATION MAP BREAKDOWN

This diagram is based on a mind map, so there is no set way to read The Musician's Communication Map. I often advise clients to refer to brand first and get that sewn up before moving onto any other area. But let's start at the very center.

Artist - This is you. This can refer to you as a solo artist, a songwriter, a producer, a band, or to you and your team. Note: if you are a band or you have a team and they are willing and able to participate in some areas, your work becomes exponentially less.

Throughout this guide, I have included **artist highlights** to bring the center of this diagram to life. The commonality among all these artists is they inherently understand the Musician's Communication Map. Some artists, like Maya Azucena, have advocated for themselves by building a strong brand based on their vision and morals. Some artists have collaborated with industry advocates and publicists to help them expand on their vision, like Joe Deninzon and Ilyana Kadushin. Eli Lev, Heather Mae, and Rich Genoval Aveo have fearlessly mastered "in real life publicity" (IRL PR) by bonding deeply with their tribes. Their stories are here to encourage and inspire you.

Brand - Your brand, of course, starts with your music. Visuals are also a part of your brand. Your choice of color scheme, fonts, logo (if you have one), photos, your single, EP, and album artwork all factor in as well. Your brand also incorporates your **signature story** which should answer the question of what separates you from all of the other musicians.

Website Copy is also included here and the style you choose on your website sets the brand's conversational tone. Break down your signature story into **shorter bios** for your social channels. And your **merchandise** is a major form of communication as it's a reflection of your brand and how your fans represent you to the world.

Social Media - Your brand immediately gets extended to your audience through your social channels, and creating a communication plan that is cohesive and interesting is an integral part of how you'll grow as an artist. There are a mind-numbing amount of social channels to keep updated and of course, each one has different parameters as far as what you include as your bio, link, and visuals. Last but not least, there's continuous updating and posting.

DSPs - Many artists overlook how they appear on all DSPs yet they are crucial as this is where fans listen to your music and may want to discover more about you. Make sure all of your DSPs have updated bios, photos, and social links. Plus, you will have to take extra steps to submit to Pandora and get in control of your artist profile on Amazon.

Ads - By now we all know that unless you are willing to pay at least something for ads you will not be visible on many social channels. Running ads effectively and testing what works is another communication channel and it will take attention and testing to get a formula that works for you.

Social Media Manager - If you hire a social media manager, you must collaborate to be sure that you are constantly checking what content performs well and what needs to be adjusted. Many people set it and forget it, but it's up to you to make sure your SMM is doing everything they possibly can to attract new fans and increase engagement and followers.

Email - Your email strategy is a critical component to your success, and the tone, style, frequency, and consistent tweaking to improve open rates and conversions should be part of your communication plan. Unlike social media channels, your email list is owned by you and is the main channel of communication to your fanbase. It is where you will ask for money.

Text Messaging - The small screens that your fans carry around everywhere they go may be the perfect place for you to be communicating with them. If you have not considered a text message communication strategy you may want to look into this as part of your communication plan.

Crowdfunding / Patronage - Along your journey you may want to ask your fans to support you directly. You have two options here: a **crowdfunding** campaign or a consistent **patronage** strategy. As the pandemic continues to ravage possibilities that artists had for making money on tour and in sessions, many have turned to Patreon to build communities and get ongoing support. A 30-day **crowdfunding** campaign using a platform like Kickstarter requires an intense amount of planned communication. An ongoing **patronage** strategy utilizing

Patreon also requires consistent and separate emails and updates on the platform.

Industry - Connecting with people who can help you in the industry is critical, and there are many areas to consider. **Networking** in general, which includes online connections, IRL (In Real Life) strategies, and email follow-up chops. A **Film & TV** strategy requires creating a way for your music to be showcased and a plan for connecting with music supervisors. And music **conferences**, which are now taking place virtually, are also a fabulous way to connect with industry professionals.

Sponsors - As you progress in your career, considering sponsorship is a smart thing to do. With the right sponsorship strategy, you may be able to get heavily discounted **gear**, get in alignment with a **brand** you love, or even get on a **showcase** at a festival or conference. How you communicate with a potential sponsor can make or break the outcome.

Media - The main focus of this book is how you will communicate with the media. Media includes **radio, blogs, newspapers, podcasts**, and **playlists**.

Publicist, Playlist Promoter, Radio Plugger - If you choose to hire professionals to handle this part of your communication to the media you will need to foster consistent communication as they become part of your team for the duration of their campaign with you. Communicating your newsworthy updates is as much your responsibility as is checking in with your publicity and promotion team to see how your campaign is moving along. And, delivering interviews and assets on time is key to any campaign's success.

This guide will focus mainly on the areas on the bottom and right side of the map - **Brand, Media**, and **Publicist**, but many of these domains bleed into each other.

3
Building Your Brand

The notion that a media outlet will cover you solely because your music is great is sadly, not true. You have to have great music and a healthy brand.

Having a strong brand ties not only into what your music sounds like, but also how you are perceived by those who have not yet heard your music.

Building and nurturing your brand means you have established:

- Your *WHY* – the reason you make music in the first place
- Your Goals – you can't build a brand unless you are building towards something
- A memorable look and feel
- A unique voice
- Consistent, compelling online content

It's vital to stick with a style that is not only true to you as an artist, but also supports how you want your fans to perceive you and experience your music.

"As the Global PR Manager for Fender guitars, as well as an artist doing my own publicity, my biggest piece of advice for independent musicians before they hire a publicist is to know their audience and who their fans are. The artist needs to have a strong sense of their identity and who their music is for, because that will guide the publicist to get the most effective coverage for them. For an artist, the purpose of publicity is to increase exposure to new potential fans, while also establishing prominence and credibility." **- Heather Youmans, PR Manager at Fender Guitars, Former *LA Times* Media Group Journalist & Singer-Songwriter**

COLORS, FONTS, LOGO AND ALBUM / SINGLE ARTWORK.

It's important to put thought and creativity into your brand, which includes your look, your photos (both official and behind the scenes / on socials) as well as colors, fonts, logo, and album / single artwork.

COLORS

Your color scheme should be consistent starting with your website. It should also carry over to your social media and any printed materials you create, such as posters or merchandise.

If you feel like it may be time to redefine your brand colors, Coolors.co is a fabulous online resource. It quickly and easily helps you come up with a custom color scheme. Once you've created a free account, you can choose from hundreds of pre-designed color palettes or generate your own. It will provide the color formulas which you can give to designers or match if you are creating artwork.

FONTS

There are a vast array of fonts to choose from, and the fonts on your website should not just be chosen randomly. They should be thought out and reflect your brand appropriately. They should also carry over to your single or album artwork and appear on any graphics you create to post on socials and merchandise.

"There are a few different types of fonts - and figuring out which one fits your brand can be challenging. Serif, sans-serif, calligraphic, graffiti, the list goes on and on. It's important to consider your sound and how you want to present to your fans. For example, if you're a jazz musician, you will probably want to give off a classic and sleek vibe - so calligraphic fonts may be better for you. If you're a rock band, you'll want a grittier, rougher feel - meaning, you may lean towards a handwritten textured font." **- Kayla Coughlan, Director of Social Media & Design, Cyber PR**

LOGO

Not every artist has a logo, but if you do choose to go the logo route it's a great way to be recognizable, especially if you stick to the same one for years (hello Rolling Stones, Grateful Dead, Dolly Parton, Deadmau5).

ALBUM / SINGLE ARTWORK

Now that we are living in a single-based music world, you will most likely be releasing several singles each year. Your brand should carry over to your cover art and should not vary wildly from your brand. If you can plan your single art well in advance you will be creating a cohesive visual strategy.

BRAND VOICE

After your colors, fonts, logo, and cover artwork have been selected, the next component to be included is establishing your 'voice.' Your 'voice' must be rooted in your signature story. Your voice may not come to you right away. In fact, it's normal for this to take time to get right.

Are you dry, sarcastic, funny, silly, intellectual, low-brow, etc.? You must consider how you develop your voice and what feels right on target with your music and with your fans.

"To cut through the noise, you definitely need to identify what's unique about your sound, your story, your background, your brand and what makes you stand apart in a very crowded marketplace. The story needs to be bigger than the music itself, something that has wider significance. Then, you will need to share it with the audience in a creative and authentic way, involving interaction and conversation with your fans."
- Delphine Grospiron, Midem Artistic & Live Music Director

WEBSITE

If you don't have a current website, you're going to have a hard time being taken seriously by the media. You absolutely need to have your own domain as it represents your shingle on the web that is fully in your control and will be indexed by Google.

The media will go to your website to check it out; from there they will look at your socials. If you are going to launch any type of PR campaign for yourself (or hire a publicist) you should have a press kit (EPK) or a press page available on your site. Many writers you pitch may search for additional information about you, and providing all of this on your website is the professional thing to do. I will get into exactly what to put in your EPK later in this guide.

Your website should be easy to navigate. One-page scroll pages are gaining popularity for their wonderful user experience. If you'd rather have a multi-page site, a navigation bar should be placed across the top of each page so visitors can see it (not buried where they have to scroll down).

Your homepage should feature your name and your pitch, or a captivating image that makes people understand what your brand is and what you sound like.

Lastly, make sure your contact information is easy to find on your website. The media are inundated with requests; if they need to get in touch and you make it hard, they will move on to another artist who was easier to get a hold of and you will miss opportunities.

"I cannot stress this enough — make sure your contact info is easy to find. That means a clear "contact" section on your website that has an email address and phone number. And it means more than just having your Facebook, Twitter and Instagram logos that hyperlink out to those sites. If media outlets have to work too hard to find you, they will give up and go on to the next band." - **Mike Farley - Michael J. Media Group & Concord Records Tour Press**

4
Getting Your Social Media House In Order

Music bloggers, playlist curators, and journalists are all trying to get more traffic to their own sites and platforms. Therefore, it will be challenging to get them to write about you (or listen to your music) if there is no proof that at least some people are already coming to your party.

Before you start any publicity outreach, you need to get your social media house in order.

"With the number of musicians and music publicists flooding the inboxes of the media, you can count on the fact that these editors and writers will be checking each artist's socials to weed out which artists not to cover. You want to have an advantage. Having a presence doesn't mean having more social likes than everyone else. It means having consistent activity online that is cohesive and engaging with fans." - **Marni Wandner, VP, Marketing and Business Development at The Syndicate**

"The first thing I'd advise for any artist to do before hiring a publicist would be to work on establishing your brand. It may seem obvious, but it's so important to be present and visible on social media these days – making sure your handles are the same across platforms so you are easy to find, having a website URL that is simple, inviting your friends and supporters to like your socials so that they are consistently growing. These are all things that will help in the long run and will be harder to change down the line than you think (trust me, I've done it)!"
- Sarah Bennett, Senior Publicist, IVPR

You should have your social media looking good and be active and engaging on all platforms regularly.

EXERCISE:
30 Q'S TO MAKE YOUR PRESENCE BULLETPROOF

This is an exercise to make sure you are present and stable online before you dive into publicity.

1.   Do you have a clean, up-to-date website?

2.   Does your website load in 3.5 seconds or less?

3.   Can you update your website easily and efficiently on your own?

4.   Are all of your URLs (names) consistent?

5. Do you have the same colors consistently on all of your social media pages (and website)?

6. Does your website include your current branding, photos, bio, music, tour dates, press, and links to your social media sites?

7. What is your Facebook Page URL?

8. How many fans (likes) do you have? Is it enough to impress a writer?

9. Is your music available on your Facebook Page?

10. Are your tour dates / livestream available on your Facebook Page?

11. Are your videos on your Facebook Page?

12. Do you have multiple, organized photo albums on your Facebook Page (how many)?

13. Do you have a tweet stream / Instagram attached to your Facebook Page?

14. Does your Twitter handle match your socials & website?

15. Does your Twitter background & header match the branding of your website?

16. Do you tweet at least 3 times a day?

17. Do you have a link to your website in your Twitter bio?

18. Is your pitch clear on your Twitter bio?

19. Is your Twitter feed available on your website?

20. Does your YouTube URL match your site?

21. Does your YouTube branding match your site?

22. Does your YouTube have featured playlists?

23. Does your YouTube have a description / bio with links?

24. Do your YouTube videos have tags and descriptions?

25. What is your Instagram account name (is it consistent with your other socials)?

26. Is your Instagram bio strong?

27. Do you post 3-5x a week on your Instagram feed?

28. Do you know how to use Instagram hashtag clouds (2-3 per post and up to 15 on selected posts)?

29. Do you post Instagram Stories regularly (at least 1X per day)?

5
Developing Your Social Media Themes

Without a cohesive narrative, you really have no social "strategy," just a bunch of posts. As part of your streamlining to prepare for publicity, you should curate four or five themes to stick to when posting on your socials. Keep the content tight and do not stray too far from your chosen themes.

"Building themes for your social media channels not only helps to create your brand and curate your content; it will eliminate a lot of the anxiety surrounding socials. With these themes in mind, you have a set plan for what kind of content to create. And once you have that, you can batch your content creation and start mapping out a concrete strategy." **- Kayla Coughlan, Director of Social Media & Design, Cyber PR**

Music is always the first theme, and then add additional topics that fit your brand. This could include your hometown, charitable causes, the outdoors, the road, etc. This way your feeds stay coherent and the media, as well as new followers, can immediately get a grasp on who you are and what you stand for.

You should choose 4-5 themes. Again, the first one goes without saying - it's your music. You chose the additional themes to fit your brand.

1. MUSIC

Releases, in the studio / behind the scenes, livestreams, videos, countdowns, news and pre-save campaigns, playlist adds, PR placements, TBT from memorable moments in your music history, etc.

2.

3.

4.

5.

As you choose your themes, keep in mind that vulnerability and authenticity are now valued more than ever. Choose themes that others can relate to and that can serve as mini-refuges for your fans.

"People are at home, spending more time online and consuming more content. Therefore, the smartest tactic an artist could deploy during their pandemic-era interviews is to shower their fans with love and gratitude, tell relatable stories, and give tactical advice or words of wisdom... talking about the music is secondary, or used to highlight the main points. By providing value within your interview, fans are more likely to share it on their own feeds or with loved ones who likely have more time to consume content. If you play it right, this next year can be the one where you build the most close-knit, dedicated fanbase you've ever had. When the economy gets moving again, guess who will be first in line to crowdfund your album, buy your merch, or support causes you endorse?" **- Clarence Charron, Founder, Pop of Colour**

6
Your Social Media Engagement

Very few people are willing to put themselves out on a limb online for fear of being judged. In fact, studies show people fear public speaking more than death. On social media you are putting yourself out "there" in a public forum where anyone can judge you, and this can feel confronting. Therefore, most artists do a crappy job of social media engagement because their posts are too bland for anyone to care about or engage with.

This is why your Instagram posts are not getting huge amounts of likes or your questions on Facebook aren't being answered.

Fans aren't always inclined to speak up.

Because of this, it will be absolutely normal for your commitment to engaging your fans to be far greater than their commitment to engaging with you. It is only once you establish yourself with the trustworthy reputation that any ideas, comments, and responses will be heard, validated, and appreciated, that your fans will start to match your commitment to engagement. Once you have solid engagement, the media will notice when you point them your way.

This means you should never miss an opportunity to meaningfully comment back and build your engagement.

"You need to have a strong and engaged social media presence — the more engaged your current fanbase, the more enticing it will be for writers and playlists to cover you." **- Angela Mastrogiacomo, Owner, Muddy Paw PR**

PART 2

Your Story, Hook, Positioning, And Pitches

7
Getting Your Music Ready For The Media

Your music is the heart of your publicity campaign. Getting accolades, plays, and notoriety for your music is the reason why you are going to embark on a publicity campaign in the first place. This means you must get your music ready for the media.

Music journalists, bloggers, and playlisters are all music lovers. They are creating and curating because of this reason. However, they can be a quirky bunch and each will have their preferences for how they like to receive music. I still work with a few writers who want physical copies of CDs mailed to them. Some like to listen to .wav files and some want MP3s. Of course, playlisters will curate their lists right from their preferred streaming platform. The more music media you connect with, the more you'll discover there is no one-size-fits-all way to present your music. That being said, here's what you should prepare:

SOUNDCLOUD

Your SoundCloud presence can be a key deciding factor in having your music covered by music bloggers.

Make sure that you have your SoundCloud profile fully built with a current on-brand header, bio, links to socials, and album and single artwork posted with each track.

Follow other independent artists similar to your genre and audience size. Heart their tracks, and leave positive comments. Not only will they appreciate it, but they may return the favor.

Before you send out any pitches, ask your fans to come stream in order to get some plays onto your profile and build your numbers. If you are going to pitch for a premiere, then set that track or album to private.

After you upload your new track or tracks, the first thing you want to do is promote your SoundCloud page to your other socials. Rounding up people who are already fans is always going to be easier than recruiting new fans, so start where you already have a following.

SOCIAL POST EXAMPLES

"We are now on SoundCloud! Click the link to stream our entire catalogue of releases. Every stream is appreciated!"

"Have you checked out our SoundCloud page?"

You can also link your SoundCloud page to multiple sections on each social network for people who might have missed the status updates.

Facebook: Link to your SoundCloud in the "About" section of your profile.

Twitter: Put a link in your bio, or link to it in the "website" section of your profile.

Instagram: Take a screenshot of your page and make it a post and a story. If a screenshot doesn't fit your aesthetic, try a funny graphic. If funny isn't your thing, try any graphic.

CREATING AND SHARING PRIVATE SOUNDCLOUD LINKS

SoundCloud allows you to create and share private links. Take some time to understand how to set these up as they will come in handy for advance listens. If you're shopping for a music publicist or sending music to industry folks, this is the easiest way to share your music for their consideration. And of course you can also share these private links with the media

SPOTIFY

Spotify has become the predominant streaming service for fans, and getting included in Spotify Playlists will be an integral part of your publicity campaign. Many music blogs have their own playlists and you will likely get included on a few just from seeking editorial consideration - it's like getting two for one!

Of course, before you get followers you must be present on the platform. Spotify does not do direct deals with artists, so you will need to make sure you have a distributor. CD Baby, Distrokid, and Tunecore can distribute your music to Spotify.

You need to build a proper profile on Spotify. Make sure to include an eye-catching banner image, multiple photos, social links, and a 1,500 character bio that is annotated properly. You also want to include links to your Instagram and Facebook as well as Wikipedia (if you have a page).

YOU NEED TO BRING YOUR OWN LISTENERS TO SPOTIFY

This is your responsibility even if your fanbase is small. Ask your fans to pre-save tracks that are not released yet; or, if the tracks are already out, request that they follow you.

There are two main reasons for this: First, to appear higher up in Spotify's search algorithm (this comes directly from Spotify's FAQ's). Search results in Spotify are based on a mix of current and all-time popularity, but vary from user to user based on personal listening preferences. The more streams and followers you have, the better your chances are to appear in searches. Second, every time you release a new track it will automatically go into the Release Radar for all of your followers. If you don't have any followers, it won't be heard.

"I know what I like, but I also know mine isn't the ultimate word on taste. If I hear a pitch that I like but don't fully get or isn't exactly in my wheelhouse, seeing that an artist has followers or tracks with a ton of plays let's me know that I'm on to something. That can absolutely push me off the fence if I'm teetering and onto the side that gives an artist or song a chance." **- Ben Kaye, News Editor, Consequence of Sound**

SoundCloud and Spotify are the two platforms where music bloggers and playlistsers will be expecting to find your music. However, they are not the only players in town. You also want to be sure you are established and have consistency on Apple Music, Deezer, Tidal, and Amazon.

8
Telling Your Story Is Crucial

t is a fact that we are living in the age of storytelling. All brands now tell stories. I like to use Tide detergent as a classic example. Several years ago, Tide commercials talked all about how Tide takes grease and stains away and featured smiling women sniffing shirts. Fast forward to today and Tide commercials show a family — mother and baby — and remind us that Tide keeps our children safe by providing safe packaging.

A quick scroll through Tide's social media show many additional story lines: Jersey swaps with the NHL, sponsorship of Michelle Obama's podcast, and Loads of Hope — washing clothes for people in hard hit areas due to storms and flooding. Many captivating storylines are at play with this brand. So, if something as innocuous as Tide can weave a world of stories, so can you.

The old music business set a standard for the artist bio. This is something you are probably familiar with — a one-page, single-spaced, typewritten bio that goes through the artist's entire history starting with something like, ..."So and so began playing music at age 3..." It then goes on to include every single milestone and accolade that the artist ever received. Even more egregious, it may also go into deep detail about every artist they ever opened for, all of the venues they played, and who mixed and mastered the album. It may also go into how the band came together and talk all about the trials and tribulations of the band members who left the band...etc. This is not a compelling way to entice fans and media.

Your bio, or as I call it a Signature Story, should tell a memorable story that the reader remembers after they read it. The story should contain a moment that stands out as THE talking point. I call this the hook.

A major complaint I hear all of the time from artists is how difficult it is to write their own bios. Many try to take it on and find it's not easy to condense their entire music careers in a succinct manner, which, as I just mentioned, is exactly what you should not be aiming to do.

There is plenty of room to share these aspects of your music history. They can be showcased on your website, or broken down into small pieces for your social media moments (hello #TBT!), but they should NOT be in your bio.

If you decide to hire a publicist, a bio may be out of her scope of work. In fact, many music publicists I spoke to for this book told me that they leave it up to their clients to provide their own bios, or they suggest a trusted bio writer for an additional fee.

Many publicists hire seasoned music journalists to craft artist biographies for their clients and I strongly advise hiring a professional bio writer. If you are not ready to pay for a bio writer, consider enlisting a fan or a friend to help you. People who are great storytellers often make great bio writers.

"It's important to have a vision of what your story is. Sometimes this isn't always evident, and that's okay. At the beginning of each campaign we make sure our clients have a strong biography – hiring a solid, well-versed bio writer is a great investment. At the end of the day, it's our job to be storytellers and to be a catalyst for others to hear that story."
- Sarah Bennet, Senior Publicist, IVP

9
The Hero's Journey

The hero's journey is shared in every single culture on the planet. It's a story structure in which the protagonist (or hero) goes out on an adventure and into the world of the unknown. There, he or she faces challenges, tests, and tribulations, and in the end comes home victorious.

This is a process that was identified many years ago by Joseph Campbell and is taught and studied widely by writers.

If you have ever seen a Star Wars, Lord of The Rings, or Avengers movie, you have witnessed a hero's journey. I recently watched the documentary Still Alive about legendary songwriter and '70s icon, Paul Williams. He wrote the music for the Muppet Movie among many other things and is president and chairman of the board at ASCAP. Paul had a hell of a journey through all of the elements described above and I suggest you watch this documentary as inspiration.

The Hero's Journey is a powerful framework for identifying what is unique and special about your story. I have created a visual way to present this in a clockwise diagram to walk you through the musician's hero's journey.

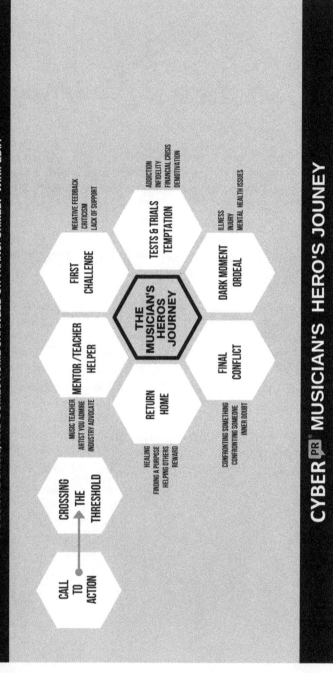

THE COMMON TEMPLATE OF STORIES THAT INVOLVE A HERO WHO GOES ON AN ADVENTURE, IS VICTORIOUS IN A DECISIVE CRISIS, AND COMES HOME CHANGED OR TRANSFORMED. - WIKIPEDIA

CYBER PR MUSICIAN'S HERO'S JOUNEY

THE ELEMENTS OF THE HERO'S JOURNEY

Call to Action

At the beginning of any good story there is a call to action. An inciting moment where you decide you love music. When you may have recognized that you must create music and perhaps you go further to identify it as your calling in life.

Crossing The Threshold

This is the part of the journey where you realize there's no turning back. I'm watching my best friend's son Andy go through this process right now. He's 15 and spends three hours a day in the drum shed he built, practicing and exploring drumming. It looks different for every artist, but crossing the threshold is when you begin to get in. Really in.

Mentor / Teacher / Helper

In the case of a musician, this is probably a parent or family member who made music, a music teacher who touched you, an industry advocate of some type, or it could be a successful artist you admire or are friends with. My friend Tania Sterl comes to mind. She was deeply inspired by David Bowie and became a fashionista and a cello player who bears a striking resemblance to the Thin White Duke to this day.

First Challenge

You don't have any family or peer support, you got some negative painful feedback, you are getting widely criticized for wanting to try music for a living as people don't believe it's a "real" job, etc. Whatever it is for you, all heros face challenges.

Test, Trials, and Temptation

This is anything that will test or tempt you. It could be something small like uncertainty or demotivation, it could be a financial crisis, infidelity, or addiction.

Dark Moment / Ordeal

This is when you may experience a turn for the worse. Addiction that gets out of control. A tremendous loss that you suffered. A mental health crisis, or something that radically changed you because you had to be in it and go through it.

Final Conflict

This is the final battle. Confronting something, someone, or perhaps your own inner strife or turmoil.

Returning Home

This could be about finding your own purpose, helping others, your healing, or how you are giving back to a particular community. This can also be about some themes in your own music and how it brought you "home" in some way.

You don't need to have every step of this journey to create your hook — just one moment can stand out to make your hook.

Here are some additional key elements to consider adding to your bio.

Music - Genre, Instrumentation, Tone, Influences

The reason you are writing your bio is to illuminate and accentuate the fact that you make music, so don't forget to actually talk about your music in your bio. At minimum, set the writer or fan up for the type of music you make so they can begin to tie that in. You can also do this by mentioning your influences and comparisons to provide context.

One or Two Achievements

I previously mentioned not to add a list of all achievements, but if there are one or two that stand out they can be included for context and they can also set the stage for telling a story.

Social Proof

If you have managed to create a voracious tribe of fans, an impressive follower count, or you have had something incredible said about you by a notable person that is funny, memorable, or otherwise stands out, it can be very powerful to include these as social proof.

EXERCISE:
EXPLORE YOUR OWN HERO'S JOURNEY

Take a good look at the 8 hexagons in the graph. Now, get a pen and paper. I suggest you write this out long-hand as working on a computer, iPad, or phone tends to hinder the flow of creating an "agreement between your brain and your hand." Pen-to-paper changes this dynamic and you may get even deeper without your notes app.

Write a few paragraphs or challenge yourself and try to write an entire page (or go on a stream of consciousness and write even more) for each of the phases of your own journey.

Don't worry if at first it feels like what I mention not to do — listing the facts and the accolades and the steps in your journey — because you will need these written down in order to hold a timeline together, but the idea is to go deeper into each one of these eight elements so that, in the end, you will be able to identify and extract your hook.

Call to Action

Crossing The Threshold

Mentor / Teacher / Helper

First Challenge

Test, Trials & Temptation

Dark Moment / Ordeal

Final Conflict

Returning Home

10
Your Hook - The Unforgettable Moment In Your Bio

have isolated some hooks for you to see, to illustrate what part of the hero's journey they match up to for inspiration and guidance.

ELI LEV

In this example you get a real feel for Eli's strong connection to why he creates music and what his mission is. If you follow him you will see that he has a knack for bringing community together and he does, indeed, make the world a smaller place, one song (and video, and Patreon post) at a time.

> *Rising singer-songwriter and global citizen Eli Lev is making the world a smaller place, one song at a time. Eli pens lyrics and melodies for everyday enlightenment — songs that resonate because they're heartfelt, earthy, and offer the wisdom he's gained through lifelong travel and self-discovery.*

> *The Silver-Spring, Maryland-based artist just released Deep South, the third album in a four-part directional series that was inspired by indigenous traditions he learned while teaching on the Navajo Nation in Northern Arizona. Just as each cardinal direction holds unique characteristics in the Navajo tradition, so do each of the albums in Eli's 'Four Directions Project.'*

FIONA JOY

This is a great example of "returning home." Fiona opens hearts to the power of music, which is deeply evident if you follow her on Facebook and see the responses she evokes from her fans.

> *When Fiona was diagnosed with Tourette's, she realized that it's often our weaknesses that give us strength. Having Tourette's taught her about life and it made her stronger. The piano, and music, became her best friend and comfort.*

> *Fiona believes that music is a gift from another world, from ancestors of the past communicating to inspire and give us hope. As Fiona shares, music is a universal language that connects us, speaks to us equally, and yet it's received by all differently. Fiona's wish is to open more hearts to the power of music.*

RENE LOPEZ

This is a "crossing the threshold" moment — you can literally smell and taste the moment little Rene decided that he wanted to be onstage.

> *Rene Lopez's earliest memories are of standing in the wings of so many stages, while watching his father — renowned salsa musician Rene Lopez Sr. — perform. Sr. played on all kinds of them – from small cramped club stages in the Bronx, to Radio City Music Hall, Carnegie Hall, and Madison Square Garden.*

> *Rene can still recall the club circuit's heady mix of cigarettes, sweat, and perfume enveloping his senses, and how the music connected the musicians to the audience, and he can still recall wanting to also be onstage.*

LANA DEL REY

This bio was crafted by Lorne Berhman and he perfectly and lyrically capturedthe genre, instrumentation, and tone of the music.

> *...Born To Die's cinematic quality is also due to Del Rey's affinity for classic arrangements. Her ability to fuse mannered torch song balladry with hip-hop bravado imbues the music with a sense of drama that feels familiar yet new. The 12-track Born To Die is*

dynamically expansive, from the rugged hip-hop flavor of "Off To The Races" to the mesmerizing grandeur of "National Anthem." Del Rey's producers and conceptual co-conspirator Emile Haynie helped her realize her musical vision, with Haynie capturing her sound in his intimate studio filled with vintage vinyl and recording equipment. Born To Die is rife with such contrasts as organic spy-movie guitars and swooning strings, grimy samples and juicy hip-hop beats.

ALI ASLAM

This addresses the "inner turmoil" part of the Hero's journey and Ali captured it so powerfully that it caught the attention of the editors at Rolling Stone India and he was featured as a debut artist - which is rare.

The Last American explores questions of identity, belonging, and perspective--not just as independent concepts but as interrelated factors that inform our relationships to culture, each other, and ourselves. The Brooklyn-based singer-songwriter's tracks find their foundation in Aslam's examination of his own identity as a Pakistani-American Muslim with a strong but complicated relationship to the mythology of American culture.

That mythology loomed large for Aslam growing up, as he straddled the Pakistani tradition of his parents and the American culture of his childhood.

These hooks stand out and can be used as media pitches and can be included in longer form bios.

"Work as hard at crafting your hook as you do on writing your lyrics. The more interesting and captivating you make it the more likely it is to be included by the media. They are looking for interesting stories to go with great music." **- Melissa Nastasi, Founder, Citybird Publicity**

11
Bio Writers Break It Down

I often get asked whether, in this day and age with social media bios being only a few sentences or a few words and an emoji, or not long-form bios are even necessary. My answer is yes. A longer bio can pack a lot of interesting punch and even though it's the hook that stands out, the longer bio still has merit, especially if you want your writer to get more backstory. Also, if the writer is an old-school journalist, they will expect a longer bio.

I asked a few writers to share their favorite bios and explain why they stand out from the pack.

Erica D'Aurora is a senior publicist at Muddy Paw PR and she founded her music blog Musical Notes Global.

BIO COMMENTARY - OUTPUT 1:1:1

Here is Erica's first commentary on two standout bios she has written. Both of her bios capture the Dark Moment / Ordeal and the Return Home is for both in the release of the music.

"What I loved most about Daniel was his vulnerability and willingness to explore his emotional hurdles through his music, so while writing his bio, I felt it was incredibly important to highlight that as a strength. So many people go through similar experiences, and I knew that storyline would for sure capture the attention of music bloggers and readers alike. Being so open about such tough topics can be very liberating for the artist, and I think it was for Daniel, but it also helps foster a sense of familiarity and relatability between the artist and writers / readers. That's what makes us love our favorite artists so much, right? When we recognize those similarities we think, "Oh wow, they're like me, they see me." For Daniel, who was releasing his debut EP, I felt it was important to establish that emotional bond between him and his audience,

which I knew in turn would help set him up to keep listeners coming back for more.

At its core, Output 1:1:1 is a project that offers a sonic representation of the toughest emotions we can experience as human beings, and the result is a very unique, avant-garde style. In bios, I think it's much more important to focus on the emotional than the mechanical, and shape a story about the artist that people can identify with. You can say this artist's music sounds like XYZ, but if you can help someone get an understanding of how that artist will make them feel, it is much more effective in helping listeners take a chance and step into the artist's world. As a blogger myself, I have received so many forms of bios that haven't told me anything about the artists / bands they're about because they focus too much on the mechanics or information that isn't relevant. As a writer, I want to know what motivates an artist, what they have to offer beyond just the definable sound of their music (beyond, for example, whether it's pop or rock or hip-hop). How they see the world and how that has influenced their work. It's important to dive deep beyond surface level in artist bios, and by doing that with Daniel and his new project Output 1:1:1, we really helped set him on a path to being received with open arms by the media and listeners from day one."

BIO - OUTPUT 1:1:1

Based in Toronto, musical project Output 1:1:1 creates a sonic representation of what truly makes us human: our complex emotions.

Although his influences include lyricists Kendrick Lamar and Laura Marling, as well as hometown heroes Broken Social Scene and legendary English rock band Radiohead, Output 1:1:1's creator Daniel Janvier employs instinct and out of the box experimentation to take listeners beyond pre-existing genre lines, pushing boundaries and journeying into exciting new aural territory. "At some point I realized how to write songs in my own voice, and not rely on the sounds and ideas my heroes already created," he reveals. "I've dealt with depression since I was fairly young, and I developed a fear that I am what's wrong with my music. I still have that fear biting at me, but I think I'm learning how to engage it in my work instead of trying to hide from it."

As a proud member of Unite Here, the international hospitality workers' union, Janvier believes in the value of hard work and is driven to help others even in the smallest of ways. Understanding the struggle of modern living and the grind of everyday life, as Output 1:1:1 he fosters a thoughtful intimacy between himself and his listeners by assigning sounds to a rainbow of emotions, awakening those that are so easy to bury and ignore and transforming them from abstract concepts into fuel to empower and enlighten.

Output 1:1:1 is currently preparing for the release of his upcoming EP Retroactive Rock Record. Recorded and engineered by Sean Sutherland, the album is an expressive and personal exploration of uncertainty, growth, and self-discovery. "I had a series of panic attacks in 2016. I started trying to interpret them through music and found my voice," Janvier said about the development of the album. "Sean was incredibly supportive during this process. His own experiments pushed the songs into territory I didn't know was possible."

Retroactive Rock Record promises to be an honest space through which both Janvier and his listeners can explore and own their emotions together, one gripping song at a time.

BIO COMMENTARY - SAINT SPICER

"What stood out to me the most about Saint Spicer was her honesty and the way she used music as a tool to learn about herself. Music is a medicine for so many, and for her, it was also a tool she used growing up to stay grounded and remain true to who she was.

I knew a lot of people would identify with her story, whether they, like her, grew up moving from place to place, or whether they've experienced another form of instability, which I'm sure we all have at some point in our lives. I wanted to position Saint as a voice to encourage others and as a source of inspiration. Someone who could help her listeners grow, help them discover their inner strength, and remind them of the importance of the voice inside that we tend to ignore but is so critical to listen to.

I also knew that her community-oriented mindset was something that would resonate with many writers. When it boils down to it, the music industry is all about community and forming and maintaining relationships, and the careers of writers rely heavily on the relationships they have succeeded in making with PR agencies, managers, labels, other writers, and, especially, their readers. In fact, without such a strong foundation in the community, the music industry probably wouldn't exist as we know it today.

Furthermore, isn't it so much better when we meet others who are like-minded and that we can not only learn from, but grow with as well? I think we sometimes forget the power of community, and what better way to receive that message than from the mouth of your favorite new artist?"

BIO - SAINT SPICER

From San Antonio, TX, to Stanford University, Jessica Spicer, aka Saint Spicer, has been delivering the truth to her listeners one carefully-penned song at a time.

Having spent much of her childhood moving from place to place, music quickly became a tool for Saint to ground herself, allowing her to express her innermost thoughts while practicing self-care by reflecting and looking inward. "I'm very thankful for music since I use it as a medium to understand and care for myself," she says.

Influenced by the artistry of innovative female industry icons like Nina Simone, Beyoncé, and Lady Gaga, Saint Spicer combines funk and soul with silky vocals and fiercely honest lyrics to convey the realities of life — however brutal they may be — with elegance, dignity, and sincerity.

Saint Spicer's ability to tell the truth has found its way into her new single "On Repeat," a contemplative track that gives fans a peek into her love life over the past four years. "When I wrote this song, I kept returning to the moments that would repeat themselves over and over again in these various relationships — getting tea together at a coffee shop, always the same taste, the feeling of the fall season and the emotions that accompanied being in love," she explains. "And then there was the actual fall, where I realized I was taking the emotional burdens of these people and carrying them with me even though there was no reciprocity in the relationship. Once you feel that betrayal, you can never forget what it feels like. It is unforgettable. And I realized I was just repeating the same process over and over again. Each fall I would meet someone new, but repeat the same process. Life is all about cycles, but I was stuck in the same one. This is the song that helped me get 'unstuck.'"

Now based in Austin, TX, Saint Spicer finds strength in the support of her fellow musicians, who inspire her to push her writing skills to greater heights. She aims to build a community through her music and believes that everyone should be celebrated for being their best selves.

Lorne Behrman is our go-to bio writer and has written hundreds of bios for our clients over the years. He holds a master's degree in Journalism from NYU and has written for the Village Voice, SPIN, Alternative Press, and CMJ, among many others.

BIO COMMENTARY - INDA EATON

There are so many angles to explore with your debut release, but what's the story with your sophomore album? For every release, including EPs, singles, and videos, you need a bio hook. Inda Eaton is a superb singer-songwriter with a robust back catalog and an engaged fanbase. For album 8, we had to think deeply about what can be said from a marketing angle. Think of it this way: if fans bought or streamed your previous album / albums, why should they buy or stream this one? Unfortunately, the answer is not based on the merits of the music.

Inda masterfully answers this query on album 8. For over 20 years, she's been an artist whose output has been defined by tours and travel. For the now-timely titled Shelter In Place (named before the pandemic), she has crafted an album narrative themed around reflective stillness. This is an album about Inda's observations while pressing the pause button. This concept is fleshed out within the bio as I weave her story, the album story, and her political and personal views into a multi-layered bio. Also, since her album was made before the pandemic, the marketing of it caught a second wind in the wake of the pandemic with the title "shelter in place" becoming a hashtag buzzword. In addition, Inda's masterful lyrics about an intentional standstill became a universal experience. What's in a title? A lot — think that carefully through. Another big lesson is do the opposite or react to your previous output as a way to shake things up for your music, your fanbase, and your bio approach.

One thing I also want to call attention to is Inda's eloquence and tact when discussing politics. We live in divided times where fiery rhetoric is the norm and we've become desensitized to it. I used a quote to open this piece because Inda's words here were a refreshing and welcoming way to open a bio. Also, these words masterfully introduce the themes of unity explored in the bio, and nicely reintroduced through the personal perspective reflected on the closing paragraph.

BIO - INDA EATON

"We can argue politics and policies, but, at the end of the day, we are bound together beyond these," shares Americana singer-songwriter Inda Eaton. "I do what I do to connect — music has this great disarming quality — it leads to vulnerability quickly as people lay down their shields."

In a career that spans 8 albums in 20 years, and a blur of endless tours, for her latest album, Shelter In Place, Inda opted for once to stay put. The 11-song record was literally tracked in the Springs, New York-based artist's backyard. In the stillness of the album writing process, she sifted through her scrapbook of travels, and created a Huck Finn-spirited collection of story-rich heartland rock songs brimming with adventure, and personal reflection.

Inda's warm humor, free-spirited emotionality, and literate flair make her songs feel as comfy as a favorite pair of jeans. Inda's vocals have a whiskey and honey-tinged raspy quality that's both stirring and soothing. Her stories and musings instantly resonate. Inda's songwriting spans fist-pumping anthems and bucolic balladeering, and it embraces a wide swath of influences, including country, classic rock, folk, and pop.

Inda's music has been a global passport, taking her through Latin America, Australia, and Germany in her early years. There, she became something of a charming troubadour, winning over audiences with her quick wit, affable onstage connectivity, and her ability to fuse rousing hooks within a down home roots-rock sensibility. These formative experiences have served her well in building an engaged following in the U.S.

Inda has toured in various configurations throughout America, both as a captivating solo performer and a powerful bandleader with a trusted posse of ace musicians. Select live highlights include opening for noted names like John Hiatt, Blues Traveler, Earl Scruggs, Hootie and the Blowfish, LeAnn Rimes, Shemekia Copeland, and Molly Hatchet. Additional performance highlights include tours for American Society of Young Musicians and VH1's Save the Music Program.

Inda has been a fixture on the CMJ alternative charts, earned an AFIM "Best Independent Album" nomination, and garnered critical industry acclaim in publications such as Billboard and Relix.

Through it all, her DIY flag has flown majestically. She has her own music publishing company, Skin to the Wind Productions, and Inda has self-produced or co-produced many of her albums.

In 2010, Inda formally committed to sharing music with younger generations in school music programs with what has become Ideas to Inspire, an arts-fostering organization that works to provide students with creative experiences through music, storytelling and self-expression. When not touring in support of her albums, Inda and her bandmates can be found traveling from one k-12 classroom to another supporting i2i programs across the country.

For album 8, however, Inda put the brakes on to ponder her winding path, thus far. "The road is a muse for me — the best way to ground ideas for me is a road trip. This album is kind of the shelter to process the trips I've been on," she details.

Besides geographic travels, *Shelter In Place* is rife with coming of age themes couched in loss. Also threaded throughout the album is Inda's multi-layered take on America. Inda was born in California and raised in Wyoming and Arizona, so one could say she deeply feels the heart of the heartland. She's also a gay woman who married in 2011.

"I do come from the heartland, and identify so much as an American — it feels like anything is possible here. We are the best chance for hope," Inda says. "I just get upset when we can't get along."

Shelter In Place opens gently with the subtle chiming guitars of "Let It Rain." The song tenderly unfolds around Inda's impassioned vocals with airy melodic instrumental textures as support. The track's spaciousness allows for a boldly vulnerable poignant short story about Inda and her mother to clearly be conveyed.

From these textural beginnings, the album winds through a vibrant array of Americana and roots rock all tied together with Inda's sturdy songcraft, affable raspy vocals, and a communal music spirit of a band playing together with intuitive musicality.

The band digs in on "Move So Fast" which features impassioned vocals and a bracing dose of heartland rock n' roll. "Initially I wrote that song about how we move fast to get a lot of things done," Inda says. "After mastering it, I realized it was foreshadowing my mother's passing. It took on a new meaning of how we move so fast as a coping strategy."

The playfully titled "What Happens On The Road" reflects on tour life existentially. The song is driving acoustic rock boasting a roof-raising breakdown. "On the road, life is kind of simple; you just need some quarters to do laundry," quips Inda. "But in all seriousness, there is always this tug and pull of reconciling home life and road life when it feels like there is no guarantee of tomorrow."

The album concludes with the exquisite piano ballad "Once" themed around a misunderstood friendship, and an almost missed opportunity to set things right. The story arcs around Inda not feeling comfortable telling a male friend of hers from her Wyoming days she married her girlfriend. When she finally tells him, his reaction was simply feeling hurt that she didn't share the big news sooner. From that moment of growth and clarity, the friendship deepened until her buddy was killed in a motorcycle accident two years later.

"That loss knocked me off my axis — it was like a gut punch. It taught me a certain magic happens when you open your heart and take a chance. Everyone has vulnerability and there is more to be gained by sharing truth," says Inda.

Inda's complex feelings of love and belonging come to life in the visual short for the album's standout "Free." Here, the rustically atmospheric song comes to life via a filmic experience that is a sweeping visual survey of America, from the industrial grit of New York City subways to the pastoral expanse of the West.

Shelter in Place was recorded at Inda's Springs, New York home with members of her longtime band, featuring B. Rehm-Gerdes, Michael Gugliemo, Jeff Marshall and Jeffrey Smith, along with special appearances by Eve Nelson, Nancy Atlas, Lee Lawler and Rose Lawler. "It was like sitting around Sunday dinner where everyone got a chance to say what they needed to say," Inda recalls of the sessions. "There was a lot of listening and seamless interplay."

Shelter in Place is a powerful entry in Inda's catalog of recorded work as it loosely summarizes the journey thus far. Pondering its resonance in her career arc, Inda says: "I feel like I'm in the best possible place to connect authentically with people. When we go onstage, there is no separation between us and the audience, we are all together. That feeling keeps me logging miles."

BIO COMMENTARY - BEN RICE

What makes this bio compelling is that there is a reimagined take on a familiar genre interwoven with a compelling personal story. In other words, music quality aside — and Ben Rice's album, Future Pretend, is exquisite — this bio flips the trusty singer-songwriter paradigm on its head.

The key hook here is the phrase "big city Americana." That description immediately creates evocative genre and personal background imagery. The reader understands Ben is working in a rootsy musical context, but he's also contributing some special elements to a genre that can often be bogged down by clichés. His metropolitan upbringing,and fresh musical influences offer a twist on a beloved musical heritage.

Another important component is the artist's self-awareness. I always believe you should make your music away from perceived marketing trends or dictates. Once your release is all tracked, then think about how your artistry fits into what's going on in the music marketing place. In these days of micro subgenres, it's imperative to be able to articulate an elevator pitch that contextualizes your music. There's such a glut of great music out there, you need a hook that tells a new listener what you sound like. In the 8th paragraph, Ben talks about his music being inspired by master chef Massimo Bottura, and he drops some tasty references to whet our ear appetite.

Here are some additional angles to consider that are addressed in this bio. Think about how your personal story relates to your music — Ben's story of nostalgia and how it uniquely relates to his Americana is a really compelling hook. Also, what themes, concepts, lyrical phrases, and emotional patterns define your music? Does your release have an overarching theme or themes? These mindsets are much more compelling than the typical chronological biographical approach.

BIO - BEN RICE

Americana isn't just cowboy shirts and twanging guitars. At its essence, Americana is a yearning for a halcyon era. Beloved cultural touchstones can be CBGBs' "the throne" door-less toilet, or it can even be that cyberspace crackle and "you've got mail" greeting you heard when you logged into your trusty AOL email account. These are as American as apple pie.

Singer-songwriter and producer Ben Rice grew up in New York City in the early 2000s obsessed with baseball and rock n' roll. He was just in time to savor an iconic run of Yankees championships, and relish Gotham's rock renaissance epitomized by NYC's fab five, The Strokes. Back then, New York oozed mystery and possibility.

Twenty years later, the city is very different. Legendary music venues have been replaced by banks and disposable retail shops. Brownstone buildings have been leveled to make room for luxury high rises. Yet, though the spaces change, the spirit lives on. Rice embraces big city Americana on his debut solo album, *Future Pretend*, an intimate and immersive pop album, brimming with ruminations on culture, society, and personal evolution.

"Over the past few years, I've seen my city and my world change so much. I've dealt with the loss of friends and family, gotten engaged and gotten to be a part of some amazing projects creatively. I knew these were all such significant life moments that it felt imperative that I was truly present" the Brooklyn-based artist shares. "We spend so much time mired in our memories, or fixated on a pretend version of reality, that we can miss out experiencing our lives as they are happening. For me, the main concept of the record is the pursuit of being present, framed by the experiences that have taken me to this place."

Rice spent his early 20s on the road with various indie-rock bands, and later laid down roots as a producer and session musician in Brooklyn, NY at his studio Degraw Sound, where he recorded Future Pretend. He went into 2020 riding high, playing guitar on a Jonas Brothers chart-topping track; co-writing in LA with powerhouse songwriters; and delving into production on a number of exciting projects. By the spring of 2020, when New York shut down for the pandemic, Rice was on the brink of a shutdown himself.

"After grinding non-stop for as long as I could remember, I was forced to take a few weeks off, like an extended snow day. Having that time made me realize how burned out I really was and gave me a moment to reset. After spending the past decade immersed in other people's music and shutting off a certain creative lobe in my brain, lyrics and melodies for my own songs started coming to me again. Then I realized, 'I have this studio that is sitting there vacant...'" Rice recalls.

At the time, New York was the epicenter of the U.S.'s COVID-19 crisis, and the City That Never Sleeps had descended into a trauma-induced coma. Broadway went dark, the subways were vacant ghost trains, and evergreen bars and restaurants closed their doors. NYC felt like 9/11 all over again. Against this unsettling backdrop, Rice made the brave trek on foot to his studio every day, walking 8 miles armed with a mask, hand sanitizer, and tissues. There, he granted himself the opportunity to create unburdened by music biz demands or defined artistic parameters. "I devised games to separate my artist brain from my producer brain, and I relied on other senses to guide me. I knew I was getting somewhere when a track conjured up smells, like rain on concrete or the damp wood in my childhood attic. I wanted the songs to be transporting," Rice reveals.

Rice was also inspired by the spirit of master chef Massimo Bottura, whose culinary creations seek to boldly evolve traditional dishes. To that end, *Future Pretend* was composed with a roots rock headspace, but Rice broadened the songs' sonic palette by sprinkling in diverse influences- Talking Heads, Echo & The Bunnymen, Frank Sinatra, The Verve, Harry Styles, and Haim.

The 9-song album opens with "Everything Changes," a swirl of cozy and reflective singer-songwriter pop replete with sleek etherealness. Here, Rice's vocals are pristinely melodic and filled with yearning, and his lyrics are impressionistic and nostalgic. On the first verse Rice sings: I don't recognize my city / Oh I must be aging / I better do something / Before everything changes / I used to walk around all day / Just to try to see The Strokes / Settle for some Two Boots / Didn't know about Rosario's. "I remember The Strokes were these mythical beings — kind of like my generation's Beatles — and I would wander around Manhattan hoping I could glimpse one of them," Rice says with a good-natured laugh.

"The Hard Road" features the lyric "future pretend," and it epitomizes the central sentiments of the album. The track's lush and transporting mix of organic Americana and electro-pop production — a thicket of melodies and ambient textures — came to Rice after a transformative trip to Budapest helped him connect with his long-lost family lineage. While there, he experienced a symphony of sounds he later recreated with his sharp production skills. *Future Pretend's* first single, the sweetly melancholic but politically incisive "American," showcases Rice's skills as an empathic writer. Here, he writes about feminism and mental health with sensitivity and visceral flair. "I grew up hearing that boys and girls can be anything they want to be, but I'm seeing firsthand we aren't as far along as we need to be," Rice says. *Future Pretend* winds down with a banger of hooky pop-rock, "One and Only," reflecting on the madness of modern-day big city living and the ever-present fantasy of escaping it, before concluding with the warmly romantic ballad, "Parade Ground" an ode to both his fiancée and to his city.

Rice wrote, produced, engineered and mixed all the tracks at Degraw Sound. He is a seasoned musician, and outside of his solo career Rice has worked as a producer, studio guitarist, and bandleader. Select career highlights include producing for Norah Jones and Valerie June; studio guitar work for Fletcher and on a Billboard #1 hit for the Jonas Brothers; playing in indie rock bands signed to WMG; and touring and sharing the stage with such artists as the Arctic Monkeys and Brendan Benson.

A solo album was a surprise gift from the pandemic, enabling Rice to make the most of a forced life pause. He says: "It had been 8 years since I put out a full-length album, and this record woke something up in me. It made me present, and it taught me if you want to do something, you have to be all in."

BIO COMMENTARY - SHANNA IN A DRESS

Shanna's bio does not quite adhere to the mold of the hero's journey but it stood out to me for three reasons: First, because it's funny and captures her spirit really well. Second, she captures what her music sounds like really well, not only drawing on sound-alikes, but also on instrumentation. And third, this bio is a great example of how to highlight accolades and achievements in a tasteful way that adds to the story of the artist because she captured her personality and her sound and tone before mentioning the achievements. They land towards the end as a way of tying the bio together and it is really effective.

I asked Shanna to talk us through how she created her bio.

"My bio is always a work in progress, I always have my ears peeled for kind comments folks write or say to me and will immediately ask 'ooh can I put that in my bio?'

Originally, in trying to nail down my brand, I sent out a survey to the fifteen people who knew me and my music best, asking questions like 'What artists could you see me open for?, What adjectives would you use to describe my music?, What colors and images come up when you think of my music?, Describe in detail a friend who you would want to bring to a show.' and so on.

Then, it was easy to see patterns emerge in all of their answers. For example, the words 'fun' and 'witty' and 'playful' came up over and over so I knew I'd use those words. Fans always tell me 'Wow! I laughed AND cried!' so that went in there. I wanted to name more famous artists to compare myself to in order to give people something to grab onto, like Ingrid Michaelson, and then I thought of the fact that I get compared all the time to Phoebe from Friends and thought that'd be fun to mix a TV character into my musical comparisons. I'll often change my trifecta of who I sound like based on the gig I'm vying for. I'll tell the older folk music lovers that I'm Ani DiFranco mixed with Christine Lavin and save Jason Mraz mixed with Phoebe comparison for audiences who have heard of him.

I want people to take away that I'm entertaining, not just a list of accolades and details of where I'm from, because I ultimately want them to read my bio, have their curiosity piqued, and want to check out a show.

My advice would be, especially if you don't have a list of people who you could ask. to read the bios of peers or people you think you're similar to and notice what seems interesting to you and copy it but madlib in your details, or even answer the question 'What do I want people to be saying about my music?'"

BIO - SHANNA IN A DRESS

Shanna in a Dress is your quirky best friend who refuses to wear pants. She says what everyone is thinking but no one else will say and you'll get an uncensored journey of clever humor and heartbreak with a hefty side of entertainment at her shows. This witty wordsmith is known for making audiences laugh and cry, sometimes in the same song. Think Jason Mraz mixed with Ingrid Michaelson with a twist of Phoebe Buffay from Friends all wrapped up in a sweet voice accented by guitar, piano, and ukulele.

Shanna started her career at the University of Virginia, biked across the country and fell in love with Colorado, and now keeps her fun music flowing out of Boulder unless she's touring along the east coast or Europe. You can't get the same Shanna in a Dress show twice with her spontaneous banter and playful stage presence. She manages to teeter the line masterfully of taking on complex subject matters with smart, yet accessible lyrics. Her songs are laden with clever wordplay and delight audiences of all ages.

Her debut record's wildly successful crowdfunding campaign reached 50% of its goal in the first day it was launched before ending up at 200% of the original goal. It is currently in production and due to be released in spring of 2021. In 2020 alone, Shanna was a winner in the Kerrville New Folk competition, winner of the Great River Folk Fest Song Competition, a semi-finalist in Songwriter Serenade, and a Grassy Hill Emerging Artist at the Falcon Ridge Folk Fest. Shanna in a Dress curates and hosts the monthly show Women in Song in Boulder, CO and tours nationally and internationally. She has most recently been seen gracing the stages of the Dairy Arts Center, Swallow Hill Music, South Florida Folk Fest, Black Bear Americana Fest, Casey Jones Music Fest, and eTown Hall. She will be on tour supporting Red Molly in 2021.

BIO COMMENTARY - THE FIRST PERSON BIO - HEATHER MAE

This bio is like Heather - honest and straightforward and it matches her perfectly. There are a few hooks here as you can read, and this very much addresses the hero's journey. Heather is highlighted later in the book and you will see this bio is perfectly onbrand for who she is in the world and for her fans.

It is unusual for bios to be written from the first person point of view, but in this case it works and it could also work for you. If you look at Heather's social media you will see this tone and style very much carry through.

BIO - HEATHER MAE

I'm a queer, fat, femme, living out loud with mental illness and v proud of all of the above. As a social justice singer-songwriter, recording artist, and producer, I use my music and my writing to speak out and build community. A few years ago, I was told I'd never be allowed to sing again due to vocal nodules. Oof. Instead of surgery, I went silent for 8-months, followed by some intense vocal coaching, and I got my voice back. I decided to dedicate my life, my career, my music, and my voice to social justice issues.

In 2016, I released my EP, I AM ENOUGH, which focuses on racial justice, feminism, LGBTQ+ equality, and body liberation. In 2019, I released my first full-length album, GLIMMER, a collection of 9 songs solely focused on one theme: mental health. I have Bipolar Disorder and a whole smorgasbord of other mental health delights, but I realized that by talking about it I was actually helping eliminate stigma and saving lives. I went on two US album release tours and sold out venues all over the country. GLIMMER was my glimmer in 2019.

When the Pandemic hit, I added two new titles to my resume: community organizer and mental health writer. I know darkness v well. Depression is an old friend of mine and community is essential in times of darkness. Since March of 2020, I launched a bi-weekly livestream called Apart Together and an online fan club — Big Loud Love Club — that gathers for virtual workshops, classes, concerts, and community events that help my amazing humans stay connected in a time of so much disconnection. I call my fans my "amazing humans" because to exist in a world that makes it so hard to do so is truly amazing. Despite everything you've been through, despite everything they told you - YOU ARE STILL HERE. That is amazing and it's my life's work to remind you of that fact.

xo, your BFF HM

This is the perfect segue to introduce our first artist highlight. Heather has become masterful at bonding with her fans and they, in turn, helped her to create an amazing community that supports each other. During the start of the pandemic, Heather got clear that she needed to do something to not only survive financially but also thrive mentally.

ARTIST HIGHLIGHT:
HEATHER MAE
How Listening, Caring, Loving, Responding, And Helping Fans Makes Magic

Instagram: @heathermaemusic

Heather Mae (she / her) I'm an alt-pop social justice songwriter and performer. I'm a queer, proud fatty femme, diagnosed with Bipolar Disorder 2, married to my hersband, Rah, and obsessed with my two cats, Sallie and Harry. I strive to write music to empower humans and make the world a better and more equal place.

I've never understood the type of musician who just shows up at the show, plugs in, plays the show, collects their money, and goes home. No fan engagement other than a few spoken words into the mic from stage and no opportunity to make their fans feel seen, needed, wanted, and welcomed. I don't understand this type of musician because, to me, that doesn't incentivize your fans to show up again. Yeah, your music was great but if I've seen it once, why see it again?

And I don't want my fans to show up for one show. I want them to show up to 15.

I don't want my fans to buy one CD. I want my fans to buy 10.

I don't want my fans to feel like they're one fan in 800,000, so "why does my support matter"? I want my fans to *know* how important they are to me because I've held their hands and told them so.

I genuinely care about the lives of the people that listen to my music. I read their messages. I know about their trauma. I know which songs of mine they listen to when they're struggling with depression, about their daughter who has cancer, their mother who is fatphobic, and their children who just came out to them as Transgender. I write to help and heal my listeners and, in exchange, my fans support the making of my music that helps and heals them.

When the Pandemic hit and my gigs were getting cancelled, I realized early on that 75% of my income was about to be eradicated. I'm a touring musician and I've worked hard over the last decade to build a fanbase in every major market. I released an album in September last year and had the biggest crowds of my entire career. And then - boom. March happened and everything shut down. I realized immediately that if I wanted to keep making music, I would have to change everything and move my entire career to a virtual one. Plenty of musicians have done this by launching YouTube series and gaining paid sponsorships from brands for social media posts. For me, I didn't have the Spotify numbers and social media following to be able to capitalize on that. What I had was a fanbase that wanted to take care of me, like I've worked my whole career to take care of them. Cue: Patreon.

There was a time in my career when I felt it was unfair to ask my fans for help. Whether it be donating to my Kickstarter, or voting for me in competitions, coming to my shows, buying my merch, or just liking, sharing, and commenting on my posts; I always felt guilty.

Here's why: an artist who always asks but only plugs in and plays and leaves is like a friend who always talks and never listens. Unless you're a narcissist, we are all aware of when we are taking too much and giving too little. Friendships must be balanced in order for them to be healthy and if you're constantly asking things of a friend, and never selflessly offering your time and energy to give and listen, well, who wants that kind of friend?

"How do I turn my fans into superfans?" I get asked this question a lot. They look at my social media and see the authentic interaction between me and my fans and between themselves and wonder if I have some secret and could I tell them. Well, yes, I do.

Be the friend people show up for. Don't just ask. Give.

Give them a space online that brings them peace and they will keep coming back. Give them resources for feeling good and they will ask you for more. Give them things that bring them joy or understanding or comfort or deep feels and tap into the parts of their brain that go "yes please, more please." Give them more than just your music and they will give you more than just one click.

I know that I can ask my fans for help because the scales of giving are balanced between them and me. I listen, I care, I love, I learn, I read, I respond, I help.

I take care of them and in exchange, they take care of me.

EXERCISE:
12 Q'S TO SHAPE YOUR BIO / SIGNATURE STORY

Today, more than ever before, having a compelling story may be the thing that attracts a writer, before they've even heard your music. So, creating a compelling story is key to attracting their attention.

Here are 12 questions to answer that will help you shape yours.

1. What genres do you play? (Be honest with yourself & choose no more than 3.)

2. Who do you get compared to? (If you don't know, ask a few friends and fans.)

3. Who are your biggest influences? (Does not have to be only other musicians.)

4. When was the moment you knew you had to be a musician?

5. How do you want people to FEEL when they hear your music?

6. Why do you play music? Do you have a mission behind why you create?

7. What's special about this album / EP? Why should fans buy?

8. What feelings, vibes, and messages do you want to convey with your music?

9. How do you define success in music?

10. What keeps you pursuing music?

11. Can you describe your audience / demographic?

12. What are some lightbulb moments along the way in your musical journey that have shaped your current sound? (describe a few scenarios)

Whether you choose a formal bio written by a professional bio writer, you pen one in the third person with a little help from your fans, or you speak directly to your audience in the first person, your bio should leave an indelible impression on the reader.

You also want to be sure you love every inch of your bio: the media will copy and paste it to death when it comes time to write about you, so be sure you like all of it since many parts will end up in your future reviews and write-ups. This is how you know you have completed this part of your publicity journey.

12
Creating Your Press Kit

Now that you have your bio you should work on the other parts of your press kit.

A thorough musician's press kit should consist of five parts: music, bio / signature story, which I just covered in the previous chapter, photos, press, or fan quotes, and videos.

MUSIC

This guide assumes that you already have fantastic music that is mixed, mastered and ready for the world. Completing your music comes way before publicity and is, of course, the reason why you are doing any publicity at all. As discussed in Chapter Seven, SoundCloud is what most bloggers want because it is easy to embed. Make sure you have professional artwork for your EP or album, and separate single artwork if you are releasing singles. You should also have your music in a Dropbox / Google Drive in multiple formats (wav, MP3 etc.) on the offchance that a writer or online radio programmer requests it.

PHOTOS

If you take this seriously, you will benefit tremendously. Create photos that are clear, well-shot, and attention-grabbing. Showing movement is a plus (sitting on a couch or up against a brick wall has been done too many times before).

Arrange a photo shoot with a professional photographer or with a friend who has a great eye and with whom you feel comfortable.

Be prepared to spend at least three hours shooting and capture a lot of shots. The wonderful thing about digital cameras is you have unlimited opportunities to capture images and you can always delete what you don't like.

Create many looks and shots using different outfits and locations that truly reflect your brand, so that when the media covers you and fans come to your site and socials, they will have a good idea of who you are and what feels "on brand."

Studies have shown that photos of people looking directly at the camera test well with audiences on socials as do photos with your mouth slightly open.

The reason you want to capture many looks and shots is that social media and single art (if you are releasing many singles) will use up a lot of your images and you will go through them quickly.

LIGHTING

If you are shooting indoors, be sure to invest in a good light. You most likely already have a ring light for livestreaming, so use it! Make sure you don't have any harsh shadows running across your face or photo.

If you are shooting outdoors, choose an overcast day or shoot later in the day so you don't get harsh sunlight and squinting in the shots.

BANNERS & SQUARES

You will also want to think in "squares" for Instagram and cover art, and "banners" to make announcements and create great social media banners.

"Since most artists pitch via email, the first thing I notice are their photos. Next, I want to hear their final mastered version of their new EP / song or album, and if they're of high quality or professionally done, then I'll consider them and read their pitch. When all the elements are of high quality, then this shows me that the artist is serious and investing in his career. With so many new artists and DJs everyday, it's easy to spot the professional looking ones from the good or mediocre.
- Francetta Evans-Anfom, Editor in Chief, Dats Muzik *Magazine*

QUOTES & REVIEWS

What you say about you is one thing, however, what others say about you is trusted in a different way. So, if you have any press quotes or media mentions, include them.

If you don't have any media quotes (yet), ask friends and fans to send you their thoughts, or you can ask them to leave their reviews on social media and websites.

Sending an honest ask is the best way to do this. When reaching out to fans say, "I am building my media kit and I would love to showcase what you have to say about my new track, live, or streamed show, or about me in general." Different social platforms make sense for different requests. If you want a review of a new track, request on SoundCloud. If you want a general quote, request on Facebook, and if you want a quote about your live or streaming shows, request on Bandsintown.

VIDEOS

Videos are a great way for the media to understand you better and get a real feel for you. Ideally, you should have a few types of videos: live performance and an official music video or two.

Select between 1-3 of your best videos and make sure they are high quality and well annotated. Keep all of these assets handy in a Dropbox / Google Drive so you can easily access them if, and when, writers request them. In addition, you will want to post them on your website in an EPK and of course have them posted on YouTube and create snippets on socials.

13
Posting Your Electronic Press Kit (EPK)

It is vital that you post an EPK on your website. The media will deeply appreciate having easy access to your information because they are constantly under deadline. You can also point other industry folk such as promoters and venues to your EPK as well. You want all press assets to be in your control so that you always have your best foot forward and are sharing the latest news, releases, and images. I don't suggest using an EPK website to host yours as you want all of the contents to count for your own SEO.

On your EPK page, post a long form, 250-word, 100-word, and a tweet-sized bio. This way, you will have created every possible type of bio request that may come your way.

EXERCISE:
PREPARING MULTIPLE BIOS

This is an important exercise to walk yourself through, as no one will ever ask you to edit your bio down again, or worse, edit it for you, and forget the most important parts.

Here are the formats of bio you should have:

Long Form

250 - 200 words

100 words

In one tweet (280 characters)

A few words (and maybe even an emoji) for Instagram, Twitter & socials

A graphic representation for Instagram posts and stories

MAKE PHOTOS, ALBUM ART & LOGOS EASY TO DOWNLOAD

Many artists have complained to me that they were featured on a blog or on a venue website with an outdated photo that a busy writer or promoter randomly Googled.

All of your artwork should be up-to-date and available for easy download. Include album art, single art, and several sizes of images.

Thumbnails are great for quick and easy loading but are detrimental for use in print (your photo may be appearing on posters, flyers, conference guides, programs, etc.)

You should always have a few downloadable photo options on your site in at least 300 dpi / jpg format. Also, post vertical and horizontal photos, and remember, square is the norm now (think Instagram). Have photos that are different ratios including square and Instagram-story size so editors working on tight deadlines won't have to resize anything.

When the photos are downloaded, make sure they are properly named with your name (not 34567902983765442.jpg) so that editors can find them in folders and on messy desktops. This will help with your SEO as well!

Create an easy-to-see link that says "click here for a hi-res / low res jpg." That way, busy editors can get what they need quickly and easily. And be sure to include album / EP / single covers and downloadable logos with transparent backgrounds if you have a logo.

PRESS QUOTES & REVIEWS

When including articles that have been written about you, never simply link to other blogs and sites. The reason for this is that the sites you are linking to may take the articles down, or even worse, the sites may go away and your article will be lost forever. Plus, you don't want to lead people away from your site. So, make sure you include the articles archived on your own site. They also contribute to your SEO.

UPCOMING SHOWS / LIVESTREAMS

If you are playing shows, you not only need a section on your site that is clearly marked, but you also need these two live show and livestreaming tools:

Bandsintown - Integrates with your website and Facebook and alerts your fans when you are playing. It's wonderful because when you update shows or livestreams, it automatically populates on both. Plus, they email fans who have chosen to follow you (known as trackers) on the site.

Songkick - You should update your Songkick account on a regular basis to ensure that all of your shows are added. Songkick feeds tour dates to Spotify, so when your fans stream your tracks, your show info will pop up for all fans who live within driving distance of that show.

Don't make your EPK password protected! A trend in the business is to have a fully "protected" EPK that is only accessible with a password. You should do this if you are displaying multiple images or links to music that is not yet released. Otherwise it's okay to have your EPK available for all of the world to see.

14
Preparing Your
Press Release

Press releases announcing that your new album is being released were standard practice in the past, but if you are seeking digital publicity, most bloggers prefer focused pitches, playlisters don't need them, and "blasting" and seeing what will stick is not a strategy — it's a fool's errand.

There are some reasons to write a press release for a very specific event, (like a show, a benefit or a special occasion), or for a very niche market (a "genre" of music is not a niche, but a charity benefit, or a tech-related news piece about you being featured in a new app, is!).

Okay, now that I got that out of the way, here is how to create a press release in eight steps.

PRESS RELEASE FORMAT:

A press release should be one page only and on your letterhead. If you do not have a letterhead, put your logo, or your record company's logo, at the top of the page.

Step 1 - FOR IMMEDIATE RELEASE

All press releases start with 'FOR IMMEDIATE RELEASE' written in the top left-hand corner, and always in CAPS.

Step 2 - Contact Information

Contact info should include your first and last name (or the first and last name of a specific person), a phone number, and an email address.

It should look like this:

FOR IMMEDIATE RELEASE

Contact: Ariel Hyatt (212) 239-8384

PRteam@CyberPRMusic.com

Step 3 - Headline

Next comes the headline, which should be simple, centered, and bolded.

An example:

2 Story Cabin to Celebrate Release of EP with East Coast Tour

Step 4 - Subhead

This is an expanded part of the headline, which brings the reader in and accentuates the headline by adding detail.

An example:

10-city tour supports *Patient Creature*, their new EP

Cities will include Philadelphia, Boston, New York,, and Hartford.

Step 5 - Opening Paragraph: Location, Date & 5 W's

Location: should start with (City, State) Date — This is so the reader knows where the information is coming from and how timely the information is.

Example: (New York, NY) June 20, 2021

And it should answer the 5 W's:

Who, What, When Where & Why

This initial paragraph should always grab the reader and answer all of the basic questions the reader might have. If the release is to promote a show or a specific event, include the full date with day included, venue name, venue address, show time, ticket price, and ages, as well as a link to the venue for further directions and information. Lastly, include the ticket purchase URL.

Step 6 - Second Paragraph: USP / Unique Selling Point & Quotes

This is the "meat" of your press release, so make it good.

This will include further information, more details, an engaging story, a quote about your music, or about the topic of the release from reviewers, fans, a producer, a venue owner, or an industry tastemaker. What other people say is always taken more seriously and is more believable than your own hype. Then, the USP or Unique Selling Point – a short description that captures the sound of the music (pretend that the reader may never actually hear it) and includes what makes you stand out.

Step 7 - Final Details & Additional Contact Information

Here is where you should include all tour dates, a mailing address, the URL to your website(s), a place where a photo can be downloaded, a link where the music can be purchased or streamed, and if you have a label contact, add them here.

Step 8 - The 3 Hashtags – The End!

Now type this:

# # #

This indicates that the press release is finished and there is not another page to your release.

When sending your press release, never blast! Choose carefully and address each writer or calendar editor by name with an intro, and give a reason why you contacted them.

15
Writing Your Pitches

Now that you have a great bio signature story, you'll need to extract elements from it to create your pitch. This takes some honing, much tweaking, and possibly some collaboration. The process of creating your perfect media pitch will take some effort. I have created an exercise to help you.

"It seems ridiculous to even say.... but check the spelling of my name before sending me something. It takes no time at all. Notes with the wrong name or spelling errors go to the bottom of the pile. The only thing worse is opening something and seeing "Dear Sir or Madam...." And be honest. Don't tell me you never miss my radio show – it's been off the air for more than two years." **- Joan Kornblith, Broadcast & Communications Expert, Folk Alliance International Board of Directors (2012-2020), Americana Music Association Board of Directors (2009-2013)**

STRUCTURING YOUR PITCH

Always start your pitch addressing the writer by first name.

Be sure to get straight to the point of who you are, what you are reaching out to them about, and be very specific about what you are asking for. Your first paragraph should be customized, keeping the site they are writing for in mind. For instance, you might want to mention why your music would be a good fit for the blog or why you personally love it.

Your second paragraph should include your basic info (who, what, when, where, why) and a description of your sound that is focused and absent of superlatives.

Be sure to include links to your website, your active socials, and a SoundCloud link to the music you are pitching (unless told otherwise in the submission guidelines).

Include any upcoming tour dates, releases, and exciting news.

Close your pitch thanking them for their time and consideration.

EXERCISE:
STRUCTURING THE PERFECT PITCH

Write Down The Following

1. Your 1-3 genres: roots, reggae, folk, punk, jazz, country, chillout, funk, etc.

(no more than two or three will actually be selected in the end.)

2. 1-3 artists (If fans like them they may like me) that other people say you sound like

3. 1-3 artists (or authors, or famous people, or places, or things) that have influenced or inspired you

4. 1-2 sentence signature story (your "HOOK")

5. 1-3 feelings and vibes you want to create or convey with your music

6. Individual assets about each song you will be pitching - What inspired you to write it? What's the meaning? What was the production like? Why is this song niche-oriented?

7. Release date, if in the future (Note: it must be a Friday)

8. SoundCloud link, site, and socials (Note: 99% of media want SoundCloud links - create separate playlists for individual songs)

9. If it is a niche pitch - The niche or niches you identified and why you fit in it (Mommy Blog, Veteran Blog, Vegan Blog, Travel Blog, etc)

Now to write your pitch, look at what you just wrote, and condense it into a few punchy sentences.

"What draws me to a band's pitch is probably different every time. After all, there is no one right way of doing things. If there were, everyone would adopt the same template and then it would lose its uniqueness. I tend to cut away at the e-mail pile based on what definitely turns me off and what is left is generally worth exploring further. Things which turn me off are many and varied but I don't want style-over-substance shots of an artist or band, be it provocative pop wannabes or cat-walk indie bands. I don't want your life history or a resume which feels like you are applying for a job. I don't want the "new" anything, and self-aggrandisement really doesn't work on me either. So, you have won a couple of battle of the bands competition...haven't we all?

But more than anything, I guess, there has to be one or two good songs in there which indicate not only where they fit in but why they are different, better, or more interesting than what's already out there. It's all about the songs at the end of the day."
- Dave Franklin, Founder, Dancing About Architecture Music Blog

CREATE MANY VARIED PITCHES

In a 24-hour news cycle where all blogs are expected to post multiple times a day to stay competitive and relevant, something very bad can happen. Overwhelmed bloggers tend to get lazy and many will simply cut and paste what you write in your pitch and will not add any of their own unique content. This makes it necessary to write several pitches, so that, if you get a lot of "copy and paste placements" they won't all be exactly the same. It takes time and is annoying to do, but when you are building your publicity portfolio, at the end of all of your effort, nothing sucks more than to have the exact same placement over and over. This will render all of your efforts moot.

Just like you did for your bio, you should prepare multiple sized pitches. These will come in handy and save you time as you begin your pitching process.

An Emoji / Hashtag Pitch: Should only be a few words and is perfect for socials like Instagram

A Tweet Pitch: Scale it down to 280 characters or less

A One-Sentence Pitch: For a calendar editor or a venue if they request

100-Word Pitch: For a journalist about to interview you, or for inclusion in a program, or on a website of a venue or livestream, etc.

Place your short pitch on your website (homepage); Facebook page in the "About" section; on Twitter - don't forget the link to your site; and on Instagram - hashtag some of your pitch for Insta effect and choose an emoji if it suits you.

Offline, add your pitch to postcards, show flyers, business cards, posters, and download cards.

16
Pitch Examples - Niche Angle, Music Blogger, & Video Premiere

"First, you need to know how to write a professional email without any grammatical errors. Second, that email also needs to clearly define who you are, what your music is about, and a call to action, such as "let me know if you'd be interested in exclusively premiering my music video." Third, you need to learn how to ask for what you want in a tactful and respectful way, but the ask won't land unless you tell a compelling story. Journalists are looking for enticing, relatable human stories, so any music you pitch should have a compelling story to go with it. As artists, music is an extension of our life stories, so make sure you connect the dots for the journalist and you'll see better results." **- Heather Youmans, PR Manager, Fender Guitars, Former *LA Times* Media Group Journalist & Singer-Songwriter**

Here are some pitch examples so you can see how we structure pitches at Cyber PR:

PITCH #1 - NICHE ANGLE

This is a pitch that I sent to a very specific niche pool of journalists and playlisters in the New Age genre. As you can see, it states that they may already be aware of the group (as they are known in this niche), and I utilized a well-known writer and publication's pull quote.

Dear (First Name),

I am reaching out today about a group you may already be aware of, FLOW.

FLOW stands for Fiona Joy, Lawrence Blatt, Jeff Oster, and Will Ackerman. It's a New Age group formed out of friendship and a history of working and playing together over eight years.

Once recording began, it became clear that Will could be an essential part of this group as an artist, as well as producer. When invited, Will was happy to join the others and FLOW was born. With Will and Tom Eaton producing, this group will surely capture the essence of today's New Age music.

FLOW has just returned from the first leg of their "Arrival Tour" where they played The Grammy Museum and the ZMR Awards, where they took home two awards for "Album of The Year" and "Best Contemporary Album." This fall, they will return to Carnegie Hall in New York.

"Every genre needs a supergroup. With FLOW, we finally have such a group in New Age music! I'm happy to report that their self-titled debut album is worthy of the 'super' tag, too. FLOW is a reminder of what made New Age music into an international phenomenon in the late 1980s, while at the same time, showing why this genre is still relevant today." - BT Fasmer, New Age Music Guide

You can stream their new album here

Focus Tracks: "Arrival," "Flow," "Waiting For Sunshine"

Find FLOW on Socials here:

-Links to Site & Socials-

If you would like to arrange an interview or have any further questions, please do not hesitate to reach out.

Thank you for your time and consideration.

PITCH #2 - GENERAL MUSIC BLOGGER

This is a pitch that was created as a general music blogger pitch. Before we sent this out it was customized slightly for each writer.

Hi ___,

I hope this email finds you in good health and spirits.

International singer and harpist, Pia Salvia, has dedicated her life to changing the function of this classical instrument by incorporating it in various styles outside of its normal realm. Salvia has an extraordinary number of accolades and has trained around the world including Belgium, France, Holland, Norway, and the United States.

A Top 20 contestant of the TV show "The Voice" in France, and Berklee College of Music graduate in Boston, this decorated musician will be releasing her upcoming album Blissful Sigh on July 10, 2020.

Currently residing in NYC, Pia shares the following when asked about this release:

Note: Here, we added a separate quote from the artist (we often ask our artists for 4-6 quotes about each song) for each of the blogs we pitched. Why? As I mentioned before, some bloggers simply cut and paste what you write without any editing. This makes it necessary to write several pitches, so that if you get a lot of "copy and paste placements" they won't all be exactly the same and you will have varied placements to share.

Please let me know if there is anything additional I can provide for you, as I am happy to do so.

With gratitude,

-Link to Music Video-

-Links to Site & Socials-

PITCH #3 - LOCAL VIDEO PREMIERE

This is a pitch I sent to Peter Blackstock, veteran music journalist at The Austin American Statesman for a video premiere. Notice how this pitch is personalized and very specific to Austin. I only needed to write and send one pitch. It landed with success and they premiered "Pieces."

Dear Peter,

I hope this finds you well and fully recovered from SXSW. After 23 years, I sat this one out!

I am delighted to reach out today on behalf of Sarah Sharp, who we worked with a few years ago when she was with The Jitterbug Vipers.

She has 2 new videos ready from her new EP "Wake" and would be honored if you would consider premiering or featuring one of them.

Sarah wanted to let you choose.

About The Videos

"Pieces"

-Link to private video-

The recording was made in Austin with the band that Sarah plays with every Tuesday at Elephant Room. Mitch Watkins - guitar, Pat Harris - bass, Masumi Jones - Drums and special (frequent) guest, Oliver Steck, on the organ.

"Pieces was filmed in my bathtub. It was all Jazz Mill's vision. Amazing what she can do with some black trash bags, glitter confetti, flowers, Crayola bath color tablets, water, an entire gallon of milk." - Sarah Sharp

"Just Go"

-Link-

The recording is just (Cuban born, Brasil-based) Yaniel Matos, on cello, and Sarah.

Shot at the Austin School of Film. The man appearing with Sarah in the video is Dorian Colbert, an Austin-based drummer who plays in over a dozen bands, and is an Adjunct Instructor of Psychology at Huston-Tillotson University, and a professor of music at Groundworks Music.

Both videos are a collaboration with Top Girl Productions (Jazz Mills) and the Lenz Twinz (Sloan and Felix Lenz). Felix and Sloan shot the videos on iPhone 7s and edited them, and Felix designed the title cards and credits.

More About Sarah Sharp:

When singer-songwriter Sarah Sharp's life began to unhinge after the passing of a beloved artistic ally, Slim Richey, instead of resisting profound foundational shifts, she bravely surrendered to the monumental changes and experienced a spiritual awakening. To commemorate this new era of fertile self-growth, she's releasing a series of four EPs in three-month increments. Aptly, she calls the opening salvo in this program Wake, which dropped on March 2, 2018.

She was awarded a grant from Austin music patron organization Black Fret in December 2017. The money she received will pay for her marketing campaign, ensuring this creatively expansive outpouring receives the attention it deserves.

As a solo artist, and a former member of the Jitterbug Vipers, Sarah has topped the Austin music award polls as Best Female Vocalist, Best Producer, Best Songwriter, Album of the Year, Song of the Year, Band of the Year, and Best Jazz Band. Recently, Paste Magazine premiered the mesmerizing single "You Don't Dare" from the Wake EP.

The EPs were recorded in Austin and Brooklyn, and capture the electric musicality surrounding each locale. Select marquee musicians on the tracks include Phoebe Hunt, and Sarah's current musical soulmate, guitarist Mitch Watkins (Lyle Lovett, Leonard Cohen, Jerry Jeff Walker, Joe Ely, K.T. Oslin, Jennifer Warnes, Abra Moore and Bob Schneider).

Sarah continues her Tuesday residency at the venerated venue the Elephant Room in Austin and makes her debut at the new Parker Jazz Club May 9th. She will also be featured on the Texas Radio Live

Broadcast on Sun Radio, from Gueros, May 23rd.

Stream her new EP "Wake" here: Link

Thank you for your consideration.

PART 3

Measure A Lot.
Cut Once.

17
Calendaring Your Campaign

All too often, artists contact me with a deep sense of urgency to release as soon as possible. After all, the project is done, and they are excited to get it out. I urge them to slow down!

Little or zero lead-time makes planning for publicity tricky and many blogs will pass you up if your music is getting old, so you definitely need to prepare lead-time for every scenario. Keep in mind you should have your target list of 25 ready before you start the clock. More about exactly how to do this is coming in Chapter 19. You will have extra added pressure once it is your release date: since playlisters and many blogs on Submithub will only take live Spotify tracks, you'll be very busy on the Friday of your release.

RECOMMENDED PUBLICITY CAMPAIGN LEAD TIMES:

Premiere – These can take time to secure. Give yourself at least 3 weeks.

More on how to get premieres in the next section.

Live Show / Tour Press Campaign – 4-6 weeks before the shows

You will need to alert calendar editors and local press with plenty of advance notice.

Online Campaign – 4-6 weeks before placements will start to happen

Inboxes are flooded with pitches, and following up three times is the norm not the exception (even for a pro team like mine) before you get a *placement.

National Campaign – 3-4 months before release

For long-lead press (meaning, for example, magazines with national distribution like Rolling Stone), the editors put their publications to bed months before they are available on newsstands. So, if your album or EP is coming out in October, you must have it ready to go, (artwork and all), in July.

Pre-Save Campaign – 30 days in advance

Playlists & Submithub – start the day of release and use daily for 5-10 days

*placement = blog post, feature article, review, calendar listing, podcast / online radio interview, etc.

18
Researching Media Outlets

There are currently over 30 million active bloggers in the United States alone. Blogs, as you know, can be about any topic. A few dozen people read some blogs, while others are read by millions. The vast majority of all bloggers create blogs for no financial gain whatsoever; in fact it usually costs music bloggers (and most bloggers for that matter) money to maintain their sites.

Finding targets that are right for you is the most important part of the publicity process. Dive in, start searching for and reading through them. The ones that resonate will appeal to you and those are the ones to target.

"Research and don't be intimidated. Many writers are open to being pitched by the artist themselves in the early stages. They want to find something new, before it's being backed by a publicist or label. Contact info for writers and outlets can usually be found with some diligent investigating online, but educate yourself on who you're pitching. Be sure to notice the type of music a specific writer covers and find the ones that have similar tastes to your style. Write a concise but passionate pitch on yourself and why your music matters. But most of all, be yourself, not what you think they want you to be. You created your art authentically, make sure that you're putting it out there the same way." **- Jeff Kilgour, VP, Media & Business Development, The Syndicate**

Take note that even when there is a submission fee involved, if you don't follow the rules of how to submit, you will be wasting your time. This is a surefire way to not get included.

"We have a small submissions fee and utilize a review board to decide on the music we play. But, in the case of Women Of Substance, here's what I have to say. "The BIG factor that helps them get chosen beyond the quality of their music is that they FOLLOW ALL DIRECTIONS. So many people don't do it. It is a constant source of frustration for us. We are actually more likely to choose a song for our show that is borderline acceptable based on quality if they follow all the directions and make our life easy." - **Bree Noble, Host The Female Entrepreneur Musician Show & Women of Substance**

HERE ARE SOME IDEAS FOR FINDING OUTLETS:

Google

A word of warning about Google: if you are just starting out, searching for "Top Music Blogs" and blindly reaching out to the first ones that pop up is, frankly, not smart. These blogs get thousands of emails a day and the chance of them even opening yours is slim to none. If you are just starting out, shoot for smaller blogs who rank lower and are likely not being inundated.

Twitter

Actively follow music blogs on Twitter and curate a list for your targets; it is possible that they may follow you back - @ them and RT to start to build relationships.

Niche Blogs

Work any angles you may have. Is the lead singer in the band a vegan, a parent, really into yoga? Is someone in the band a video game junkie, or an aspiring travel writer? Pitch to a few blogs that cover these topics. A musician on a blog that is not only covering music is like a shark in a sea of tuna. You'll stand out, and that's what you want.

If you are thinking that you don't want to be pigeonholed as the "gluten free rockstar," please understand that this is only a tiny part of who you are as an artist. Honing in can open up a world of new fans and contacts, allow you to travel to tour stops, and participate in niche opportunities you haven't even dreamed of yet.

Guest Blogging

Many blogs have open call-outs to writers who want to submit their own posts. These are known as "submit your story" or guest posts. These could be a very good option if you enjoy writing and you have a story that you want to tell that will fit well as a guest post. To find "submit your story" blogs that are relevant to your niche, Google your appropriate niche (i.e. mental health, world travel, positivity, anti-bullying, whatever niche that relates to you and your music), plus "submit your story" or "submit a guest post." Make sure each blog is active.. Look to see that the blog is regularly updated with frequent guest posts, or your post may not go live in time.

LinkedIn Blogging

LinkedIn allows you to create your own blog posts. This can be an extremely effective way to get your message in front of your LinkedIn community, which is in many ways spinning your own PR wheels. If you are active on LinkedIn and you have a music related blog post it can, in turn, be shared on your group pages.

Podcasts

Just like with blogs, forge relationships with podcasters by listening to their shows and leaving comments and reviews. Podcasts are available by searching Google, Spotify, Stitcher, or Apple Podcasts and there are many that feature independent artists.

Musicsubmit

Musicsubmit (musicsubmit.com) - This site features a large swath of online radio and smaller blogs. You start by uploading your music, photos, videos, bio, press release, and social media links. Next, choose a submission package and your music and bio will be submitted to a combination of radio stations, online music magazines and publications, blogs, and podcasts. You can opt in for a monthly subscription or buy packages.

SubmitHub

SubmitHub (submithub.com) is a portal where you upload your music to share songs with music bloggers, record labels, radio stations, Spotify playlisters, and YouTube or SoundCloud channels. This site is run by the founder of IndieShuffle which is a music blog. WARNING: This platform tends to take music that is very trendy on popular blogs (Indie Rock, Chillwave, Hip-Hop, Electropop & EDM). Most submissions are rejected - look at each blog very carefully before you spend credits, and be warned: each outlet gets paid to send you feedback and some of it can be a bit harsh, as many of these sites get hundreds of submissions a day and they quickly move through submissions. The upside is you are paying for feedback ($1 per blog / outlet submission) and if you submit to enough you will get placed. Also, you can find really great people here who you can build relationships with who will support you for many releases to come once you learn the platform.

Fiverr

Fiverr (fiverr.com) is a vast site that has endless entries and you can find music reviewers in the mix. This is "paidvertorial" (meaning you are paying for a review), but there are some thoughtful reviewers on this platform and a few bloggers we have been pitching for years are here. Search for "Music review," "Music Blog," "Music feedback," and play around to see what you find. Reviews can cost between $5 - $25

Fluence

Fluence (fluence.io / list / promoting-to-music-journalists-writers-and-bloggers) says this on their site: DIY PR: send your music directly to curators, bloggers, and other trusted sources. Get feedback from people who want to help you promote your music. You can pay by the minute or a submission fee, depending on the outlet.

Musosoup

Musosoup (musosoup.com) is a UK-based site that has a list of many pay-to-play blogs. This costs more than the other sites but it will save you time by connecting you directly to higher quality blogs then you might find on Fiverr by sifting through the hundreds of options. A feature here is approximately $20 USD.

Chartmetric

Chartmetric (chartmetric.com) collects music and artist data from many sources and makes it easy to find all Spotify playlisters along with their links to socials. They also have tools that can help you compare yourself to other artists on Facebook, Instagram, Twitter, Bandsintown, Spotify, and YouTube. They have a free version and a per month ($140) fee. If you are going to do hardcore research I suggest the premium version.

Women of Substance Podcast

Women of Substance (wosradio.com) is for women and female-identifying artists. This show has "themes" as well as regular variety shows, and you can submit for either. Submit your music directly on the site for around $9 - $18.

"Build those relationships! The big secret to PR is that there's no real secret. With enough time and effort, anyone can write a pitch, put together a press release, or find contacts. The key is in the relationships. Do you have the time and energy to really invest in building relationships with writers, playlisters, and influencers? Because, if you and I write the same exact pitch and send it at the same time to the same writer and I have a relationship with them and you don't — guess who is getting that feature?" **- Angela Mastrogiacomo, Owner, Muddy Paw PR**

19
Curating Your Targeted Media List

The music publicity process for all musicians – no matter how big or small – is very much the same. Of course, the size of the outlets in which you receive placements will vary

Part of the art of being successful at publicity is taking time to understand who you are pitching. This is what will separate you from the hundreds of other artists who are also vying for placements.

Before you send any pitches, be sure to first spend quite a bit of time getting to know and understand each outlet or writer you are targeting. This means you have to take the time to read the blogs and get a sense for the tone, style, frequency of posts, and contributors. Most blogs have multiple writers who cover different genres or regions, so be sure you identify who is right for you. Many music blogs have an "About" page that will show exactly what each contributor prefers and how they best like to be contacted. Follow each writer individually on all social media platforms. A Google search will help you as the blogs may only feature their own socials, but each writer will also have her own. Once you find the writer, like, comment, tag, and contribute. The key here is to listen and connect before you make an ask.

"Do some heavy research on the publications you hope will cover your content. Looking for reviews of your new album? Read a lot of album reviews and take note of who writes them and research the writers. Look up the list of a magazine or website's staff writers, find them on social media, and follow them. Absorb their content, but most importantly, engage with it. Don't just like a photo or watch a story - comment on it, react to the story, begin a conversation around the content. Show that you respect and know their work as much as you want them to know and respect yours. Once the general lines of communication are more open and familiar-feeling, they'll be more likely to respond if you ask to email them to invite them to a show, let them know you just finished up a new music video, or anything else. Don't be shy!" **- Amanda Bassa, Publicist & Freelance Writer for HipHopDX, XXL, The Source**

Writers and editors are savvy and they can read through an inauthentic pitch. Don't cut corners, and do the work!

"We get it. You are pitching your music to dozens of blogs, and that is fine. We also know that you read the dos and don'ts and learned to compliment a blog. However, when you write something like, "I'm a big fan of the blog, and I follow your blog for a long time, and I love what you guys are posting," then this does not sound authentic but impersonal. At the very least, replace "blog" with the blog's name. Don't just mention one of the most recent songs but an artist or a song similar to how your music sounds.

In our specific case, every artist who writes our blog's name correctly - glamglare - already makes us more interested. Even better, if you clicked on our "About" and addressed us by our names. It shows you spent at least a moment and want to really get a write-up out of your inquiry. Makes us also most likely reply to you when it comes from a personal place.

My advice: Be personal, be authentic, spend a few minutes on each pitch because these extra minutes will make a difference."
- Elke Nominikat Executive Editor, glamglare

CREATE YOUR LIST OF 25 TARGETS

Your list should have quite a bit of variety including a few bigger outlets – these are your stretches. You might as well aim big on a few, because, if they come through, it'll be a great win for you. However, don't spend all your time pitching to big names because when you are starting out, it's the small and medium blogs that are going to feature you. Make sure to include a podcast or two on your list, as well as a few niche, non-music blogs, if applicable. The team at my agency has placed countless posts and guest features on blogs that cover travel, parenting, anti-bullying, and even being gluten free. I would also encourage you to try for some traditional long-lead press as well, like a magazine, newspaper, or TV show in your area that makes sense for where you are in your career.

Don't be afraid to aim big but also be realistic. Don't expect to be covered by top-tier publications when you're starting out. Focus on indie blogs and build relationships with journalists and / or editors at such outlets.

"When you're starting off, aim for multiple low- to mid-level features rather focusing your energy on big publications. If you land something big, that's incredible but don't be disappointed if it doesn't happen immediately. And remember, followers on social media don't define the reach or quality of a publication!" **- Malvika Padin, *Clash* Magazine, New Musical Express (NME), Gigwise, *Nottingham Post*, The Line of Best Fit, EARMILK, *The Voice* (UK), Gal-Dem, The Nerd Stash, *1883 Magazine***

Search for posts and articles about artists that sound like you. If you're always getting compared to a certain artist, research who's covering them. Search blogs for other artists you know and play with. To do this, first write the names of 5–10 artists that you know and play with that match your genre. Then, search for them.

Stay away from huge names like Drake or Bob Dylan. Search for artists who are smaller and have a tight niche audience. I recommend artists who are 1-3 years ahead of where you are now.

EXERCISE:
CREATE A 7-STEP PLAN FOR EACH TARGET

Yep, a plan. Here are the 7 steps that you will need for each one. I suggest you lay these all out on a spreadsheet or a Google doc so that you can keep track of where you are at any given time with each target.

One of the reasons I became a highly successful publicist placing features for thousands of artists was because I kept a database of all of the conversations I had with each writer. I would make notes about what they liked and what they didn't and what they talked about with me. And I would also keep track of who they were writing about.

1. The name of the writer or editor (first and last if you can find it)

2. Where that writer lives (this will be relevant if you are touring and want live coverage)

3. Social media links - follow them across all channels

4. A band, or artist, or topic (or many, preferably) that is the impetus for why you are reaching out

5. A few sentences / observations about why you have chosen their outlet and why you think you may be a good fit for them, including what you want from them!

6. What you are pitching (a song, a video, a premiere, the full EP, etc.)

7. How the writer likes to receive pitches / how often should you follow up, etc.

"When sending emails to media contacts, be upfront about what you're asking for. A single / album review? A premiere? A feature? Then answer this question: "Why should they care?" Besides a short, killer description of the music, provide concrete evidence of any engagement happening to date including impressive streaming or view numbers, existing reviews or coverage, radio play, etc. Any notable players or collaborators on the track?" **- Brendan Gilmartin, Publicist & Founder, Chart Room Media**

"I always notice the pitches that make a little bit of effort to tailor the pitch to each recipient. I understand that you are probably sending lots of emails out, but taking just a little bit of effort to personalize your message for a recipient can go a long way in improving your conversion rate. If I see that an artist took the time to learn a little bit about me and what I do, I am much more likely to reply back.

If the pitch is not coming from a publicist that I know (and trust), then I need the artist to make an even bigger effort to create an authentic connection in their pitch. If the artist is a complete stranger and doesn't have a publicist, then that artist should really go out of their way to create a more personalized pitch for me so that I can get to know them. And if they expect me to want to learn more about them, they definitely need to show that they took the time to learn more about me and the work that I do. Also, don't make it difficult for me to learn about you. Make the pitch concise but informative, and make it clear how we might be able to help each other.

An artist once wrote me an email where they had told me that they read my book and listened to several of my podcast episodes. They wrote to me about specific insights they gained from the material and asked me additional questions that popped into their head afterward. Based on their review of the material, they then gave me specific, actionable pitches in their email for how we could help each other. It was awesome!"
- Ryan Kairalla, Host, Break The Business Podcast

PART 4
Launching Your Publicity Campaign

20
Sending Media Pitches

f you've followed every single step so far in this guide, you should now have everything you need to start sending your pitches. Getting that first feature can feel intimidating but you have your pitches, your target list, and your 7-step plan for each, so now it's a matter of staying organized and diving in.

"It's the little things really, and they generally are not in the pitch itself. They happen way before that. I take notice when artists are supporting our mission on social media and tag me. Maybe they share an episode with their friends and mention a takeaway they had or something new they learned. Maybe they write a review of the show on iTunes and send me a screenshot in a DM thanking me for the work we do. What really impresses me is when people do their research on the history of our platform and my career. I've had some artists tell me they visited my personal music website and loved a specific one of my songs. It's not about stroking my ego as much as showing they took the time to check me out and see if we have common ground. That tells me they are hungry, and that they are the kind of artist I want to support by having them on the show... The other major thing that piques my interest when reading their pitch is when they present me with a gap in our programming that they can fill. I've had people come to me and say that they've reviewed our show and although we have episodes covering x, they didn't find any covering it from a particular angle. So number one. they've done their research. Secondly, they're going to provide new value to my audience. And thirdly, they're making my life easy by providing potential

talking points. Be sure to make the pitch succinct and get to the point quickly. For anyone receiving pitches, time is of the essence. In my case, my assistant is seeing them first and she goes through a lot of emails so she needs to see the value to our brand up front or she won't pass it on to me" - **Bree Noble, Host The Female Entrepreneur Musician Show & Women of Substance Podcast**

"Invest in relationships. Identify playlist curators that you think are going to be around for a while and get to know them. Maybe not pitch them anything to start with - maybe just stalk them a little on social media and share / comment on some of their posts. Early stage curators see this and they are appreciative of it. Once you establish a loose relationship on social you can move that up by reaching out directly on email - again - maybe not pitching them the first time but establishing a dialog. Once you've shown the curator that you are prepared to give them some of your time then it makes it easier for them to give you theirs.

The trick here is identifying who is worth targeting. I would posit that independent curators are going to play an increasingly important role in the future of music discovery - if you can develop relationships with them at the beginning of their careers it is going to have a huge payoff over time." - **Paul Sims, Playlist Curator, Music to Shake a Hoof on Musicto**

PITCHING VIA EMAIL

"Take emails seriously. The artist introduces themselves but keeps it on point – no need to re-write a bio here as that's what the About / Bio section of the website is for. The email includes every link to the artist possible - website (and bio), social media platforms, YouTube / streaming, etc. - in easy reach so we don't have to look them up. In general, outlets are busy and their time is valuable, and doing this allows an artist to stand out among the massive amounts of emails.

They also must include either a current song or a sample of their work early into the email. Most of the time that's listened to before (or during) any of the email is even read. Including it early on also shows the artist is confident in their work. While the body of the email may be the cover letter, the track is the interview. An artist may never have opened up for any big names or played a festival, but they have the talent of a headliner and that will only be known if a sample is heard. And visa versa – someone may have an impressive lineup of gigs but when you listen to the sample, it just doesn't click. (Also, it helps us to determine if an artist fits in our niche - country).

A huge pet-peeve is when a pitch comes through that is obviously not anywhere near the genre we cover – which is clearly stated in our name. Folk, Americana, rock – ok there is a chance that the genre lines could be blurred – but punk or deathrock? Not really. It shows that no research or effort was made, the email was sent totally blind and honestly, it wastes time on both sides." **- Janeen Megloranzo, Writer, The Country Note**

When you are crafting your pitch be sure you are careful to not create a copy and pasted template. The media hate this and they will see right through you.

"I've never seen a template that didn't look like a template - and I don't like templates. You're competing for my time and when you use a template it just says to me that you don't value my time. So a few super basic things that will ensure I at least look at your submission:

- *Use my name - seriously - you'd be astonished by how few people do that and therefore how noticeable it is on a submission when I see it*
- *Reference other tracks on my list - give me the sense that you've at least looked at the list and are confident that your track could be a good fit*
- *Be upfront about your digital visibility and let me know which platforms you will promote my playlist to should you be added.*

The point here is that we're trading time - my time to listen to your track and then choose to write about it against your time spent sending your track off to different playlists. If you don't value my time - if you don't give me a little of yours - then it's an unfair trade and I won't engage. And believe me - no matter how great your track is - there are literally thousands of other tracks with similar themes and production values competing for my ears." **- Paul Sims, Playlist Curator, Music to Shake a Hoof on Musicto**

IF YOU DON'T HAVE A NAME - DON'T SEND THE PITCH

Sounds a bit harsh right? It's not. Competition is fierce, and going the extra mile to take this whole publicity game seriously is what will produce results. I've heard from dozens of writers and editors who've mentioned how much they despise it when emails are not personalized and how that's a surefire way to get moved straight to the trash without further consideration. Here are two quotes that drive the point home:

"A personalised email really makes my day and I'm far more inclined to reply to them. I get a good mix of people who have simply picked up my email from online and sent a generic mailout regarding a release. It often makes it seem like spam rather than an artist trying to establish a connection, so my spam folder is where these emails end up as well. **- Malvika Padin,** *Clash* **Magazine, New Musical Express (NME), Gigwise,** *Nottingham Post,* **The Line of Best Fit, EARMILK,** *The Voice* **(UK), Gal-Dem, The Nerd Stash,** *1883 Magazine*

"Having gotten my start in the music industry as a blogger, I have been on the receiving end of thousands of pitches, and I've seen many that just shouldn't have even been sent out in the first place. At least 75% of them are not personalized, and quite a few are even addressed to BCC (yikes!).

I can assure you that most writers will be much more likely to respond when they see you've put effort into your pitch and that you're not just sending out a mass email. Personalized emails trump unsolicited press releases any day of the week, so instead of sending out a mass press release, take the extra few minutes to craft the perfect pitch. It's worth it! **- Erica D'Aurora, Publicist, Muddy Paw PR & Music Blogger Musical Notes Global, The Honeypop**

PITCHING VIA FACEBOOK, INSTAGRAM, OR TWITTER

A pitch you are sending via Facebook, Instagram or Twitter will be considerably shorter than the pitch you sent through email. This is why I suggested you write several size pitches to have at the ready. If you're pitching a writer's personal account it's imperative that you be polite and respectful. Briefly state your reason for reaching out, describe your sound / important facts, and include links to your SoundCloud and your website.

Direct messaging a writer or music blog on socials can be a really effective way of following up on an email you never got a response to even after following up via email several times. Not every writer will like this approach, so testing this is key.

"A few people have messaged my Facebook page directly for a review. This puts a face to the name and, although some bloggers will tell you they prefer not to be bombarded, sometimes it can work in your favor." **- Ilana Held, Editor, VOIDD Music Blog**

MAILING PRESS PACKAGES

There are still quite a few writers and outlets who prefer receiving physical packages. If you don't have a physical product you won't be pitching this way, but if you do and you are trying to get the attention of long-lead press, radio, or TV, the good, old-fashioned press kit and press release will come into play here. I know I have said that you should not write a press release for an album or an EP and this holds true for digital pitching, but there are still some very traditional outlets - especially classical and jazz - who will expect a release. The best way to research that is look at other artists in your genre and see what you can find on the public relations firms' websites who represent them. It will be obvious if you need to write a release by what you can find posted.

"I still get a lot of packages to review each week. The ones I get to first are from people I know and respect. After that, I open the ones from people I know and don't respect. Those are followed by items from people I've never heard of before. The packages that go to the bottom of the pile are the ones I can't open easily. So, when faced with a million options, don't go for the plastic mailing pouches that require a knife (or scissors) to open. Next on the "do not like" list are the cardboard ones, mailers filled with packing materials that fly out in a million pieces when opened. The stuff that looks like insulation. Those are also near the bottom of the pile. **- Joan Kornblith, Broadcast & Communications Expert, Folk Alliance International Board of Directors (2012-2020), Americana Music Association Board of Directors (2009-2013)**

If you are sending physical packages, give yourself plenty of lead time (at least a month) and check with the writer before you send anything to be sure you are sending what they need. If you can get in touch beforehand it will save you a lot of wasted packaging and effort.

"Think hard before putting something in the mail. Ask yourself why you think I might be interested in your project: Does it sound like anything you've heard me play on the radio? Have you heard or seen me review something of a similar style? Have I talked about the subject matter or expressed an interest in something remotely related? Did someone tell you they'd talked with me and I'd said send it? Do we have any friends in common? Have we met? Have you heard me speak anywhere? Do you have any reason to think I'll like your project, other than your mother said I would (and I don't know your mother!)? If the answer to any of those questions is NO, think twice.

If the answer to any one of these questions is YES, come up with a reason why you think this project is something I need to hear. How would it benefit both of us? Write up an argument. Check your spelling and grammar and go for it. But spend your time and money wisely, especially at first. Don't send your songs to every radio station in town – they won't play them. But your superfan with a podcast will." **- Joan Kornblith, Broadcast & Communications Expert, Folk Alliance International Board of Directors (2012-2020), Americana Music Association Board of Directors (2009-2013)**

FOLLOWING UP

It's critical that you follow up. Most musicians never follow up at all. At Cyber PR we follow up with outlets three times before we stop and move on and I suggest you do the same. Be careful though, there are some music blogs that state in their submission guidelines to never follow up. If they don't want you to follow up, they will make it clear. This is why it's crucial to get to know who you are pitching and what their preferences are, and add this to your 7-part plan.

"Two P's: be PERSISTENT, but be POLITE. Assume that the person you're contacting receives hundreds of emails and countless calls a day, and use that to inform the way you approach them: you don't want to get lost in the deluge of emails and voicemails, but you also don't want them to start to dread hearing from you. Be pleasant, polite and to the point, and don't be bummed if they don't have time to talk with you. Offer to send or resend materials, tell them how much you appreciated speaking with them in your follow-ups, and do follow-up every week or every few weeks or so, to stay on the radar but also to give a little breathing room. (I've had folks

follow up with me politely for almost a year before I was able to give them any coverage.)

Also, make your materials as user-friendly as possible: Imagine this scenario: the editor is on deadline and just lost a story, and needs to fill a quarter page with something interesting. If your materials are attractive, well-written, spell-checked, grammatically correct, and concise and to-the-point, with easy-to-access music links and high-res images, you make it *that* much easier for your release / event / fundraiser / etc. to be used as last-minute filler. (It doesn't happen often, but it DOES happen!)" **- Kristin Fayne-Mulroy, Managing Editor / Arts and Entertainment Editor** *The Amsterdam News*

1-2-3 STRIKE & STOP STRATEGY

If you use Gmail, there's a fabulous reminder tool called Boomerang which will keep your follow-ups organized. Once you send a pitch, you can schedule reminder emails to yourself. If the email was unopened it will come back to you to send again. Stick to the three strikes and stop strategy (meaning send the pitch three times). If the writer doesn't respond, try one last time via social media (only ONE social at a time) and move on.

"Do not be offended or take it personally if someone you are trying to get in touch with doesn't email you back right away; especially if you are trying to get a hold of someone at a bigger outlet. Depending on the size of the outlet, some editors & writers are getting hundreds and hundreds of emails in a single day, so it might take some time for them to get back to you. Follow-up, but if you don't hear back after a few emails, consider it a

pass. I feel like a lot of people searching for new music in the current climate enjoy visual stimulation along with the audio; highly recommend having some well put together videos to go along with singles." - **John Cohill, Publicist, Force Field PR**

BE CONSISTENT

As they say, Rome wasn't built in a day. You will most likely be releasing several singles over the next few months, so keeping consistent with your publicity outreach is key. A lot of writers and playlisters on Submithub have told me and my team that even though they didn't accept the first track we submitted from an artist, to please keep sending. This is encouraging, so be sure to make notes about who to re-send your music to the second, third, and fourth time around. Make sure to refer to your 7-part plan and track everything.

"Work on five new media outlets a week. Follow up with a new photo or story in a few weeks. Every few months, follow up with some of the more encouraging indie outlets and radio." - **Anne Leighton, Publicist, Ann Leighton Media & Music Services**

BE HUMAN

When I put out the call to writers when I was editing this book I was flooded with many wonderful responses about what actually works. I loved this suggestion from Matt, a playlist curator from Music.to.

"Here's something I've never seen an artist do, and yet I can guarantee it'd get me to sit up and take notice of their submission: not even pitch me a track at all.

Sounds a bit counterintuitive, but hear me out. Curators, unsurprisingly, are humans, and humans use all kinds of psychological shortcuts to get through the day (smarter people than me call these 'heuristics'). When curators are used to receiving a high volume of submissions, they'll use shortcuts to filter out the noise, because listening to everything would leave them with no time to do anything else and despite what people think, we aren't machines! I say this because a lot of submissions read like they weren't crafted with a human recipient in mind, and this can be a surefire way to trigger the 'do not listen' heuristic.

Instead, send an email that reaches out not as a potential playlistee, but as a potential friend. Ask them what they're interested in, why they got into playlisting, what they do in their spare time. Just take a genuine interest in forging a real human connection, and make an effort to get to know them. Instead of rolling the dice on the whims of an individual you know nothing about and merely hoping your pitch has enough to trigger that particular person's 'do listen' heuristic, eliminate the doubt entirely by building to a point where you can just ask them. Use the often-cited yet rarely-helpful 'everyone's different' adage to your advantage.

The take home from this? Craft friendships, not pitches. Because where you're going, you'll need as many friends as you can get." **- Matt Jenko, Playlist Curator, Music to Escape Reality Playlist on Musicto**

BE PATIENT

Publicity is a slow-moving vehicle that can take time to get results.

"The best advice I can give is to not get discouraged. I've often compared freelancing, and its continuous pitching, to dating – you're going to hear "no" a heck of a lot, but it's not a reflection on your work, or who you are as a person. Sometimes what you're offering up just isn't what someone is looking for at the moment. This same ideology applies to an artist pitching themselves to press. Some days will be brutal, but that's when you have to look at the bigger picture – OK, the day sucked, you heard "no" a few times, and a bunch of people ignored your email ... but how's your week been, or your month been, or your year been? Remember to keep in mind it's a journey, and to have a longview of your career. It's all about perspective."
- Adam Bernard, Veteran Music Journalist, Adamsworldblog

"Don't give up if no one's taking the bait — just develop and adapt. Look for what makes you special and unique and play it up. Polish your branding and social media to fit together. Work on your album artwork and your production style. These days, fitting into a genre is important, so try to figure out what other artists you sound vaguely like. And, of course, hone your songwriting. Songwriting is everything!" **- Ilana Held, Editor, VOIDD Music Blog**

Way back in 2010 I had the pleasure of working with an artist who was eager to learn everything I was blogging about and teaching at the time. I taught Manafest that his email list was one of the most valuable assets he could build, and all these years later he has a massive list that helps him to make an impressive income as an artist and a coach for fellow musicians looking to create sustainable livings.

ARTIST HIGHLIGHT:

CHRIS GREENWOOD AKA MANAFEST
Shares His 3 Top Strategies For Guaranteed Publicity & Radio Placements

Instagram: @manafest

Hi, my name is Chris Greenwood A.K.A Manafest. I'm a singer, songwriter, rapper, author and skater. I write rock, rap, and pop music, carefully assembling experiences and compelling inspirations that speak to a wide variety of fans across the globe. I've garnered four JUNO nominations, multiple GMA Dove nominations and a slew of GMA Canada Covenant awards. My music has been featured in the NFL, video games, throughout television shows such as Knight Rider, One Tree Hill, and MTV Unplugged, and most recently in the movie Hard Target 2. I've sold over 500,000 albums worldwide, performed over 1,000 shows across 4 continents and currently have over 430,000 monthly Spotify listeners.

I am a guy of no fluff and I like stuff that works. I know sometimes it seems easier to just delegate your marketing or publicity to someone else expecting them to win you the world. However, I've learned that you can't expect unless you first inspect. I want to share with you a few strategies and lessons that have helped me with publicity and radio.

1. Plan Ahead

When emailing someone for publicity or to get on the radio, plan months ahead. Keep the email super short and do not share your life story. 1-2 paragraphs at the most because people don't have time and are constantly being bombarded with emails from wannabe artists. Never ever send an email with an unsolicited attachment, always send a link to your song via Dropbox, YouTube or Spotify etc.

2. Always Follow Up (a lot!)

Once you've emailed a blogger, manager, radio station or whoever you are trying to get the attention of don't think your job is done yet. The secret to getting any success is the follow up and when someone closes the door you've got to learn to keep knocking until they answer. I had to email this one radio station 5 times before I finally got a response, which in turn got me the add. I had emailed this radio program director 4 times already using a software called Active Campaign so I can track whether or not someone has opened or clicked on the song link. This helps me to be strategic in how I follow up with people. I noticed this guy Mike at the radio station had opened some emails and even clicked on one so I know he's getting my emails and perhaps he even listened to my song. However, people are busy and you are not their priority as much as you think you are. While at the park playing with my daughter, I thought to myself, I'm just going to resend the same email again to this guy but change the subject line to see if he responds. I put his name in the subject title to get his attention. Sometimes, if someone is not responding I'll even get a little obnoxious and use "Yo!!" but be careful cause you could tick some people off. Long story short, Mike responded to me almost instantly apologizing, while telling me he not only added the song but would like to interview me. This is the power of following up and being relentless about your music career.

If I can't get a hold of someone via email, I will look them up on Facebook, Instagram, LinkedIn or anywhere else I can find them. I will find the phone number of the radio station and leave voicemail messages.

21
To Premiere Or Not To Premeire?

A few years ago, music blog premiere was a buzzword in the music publicity space. Many musicians wanted to get their tracks premiered on music blogs and there was a feeding frenzy around getting them that made it a cut-throat proposition. Today, as you are researching music blogs, you will still come across sites that run premieres.

For emerging artists, premieres are often revered as some sort of magical key to unlocking popularity. However, few artists who ask my publicity team for them understand exactly what they are, how to get them, and the reality of their value in the grand scheme of things.

A premiere is, sadly, not a solution to gain massive atention and plays. It's offering a blog exclusive content (i.e. a track, music video, album stream) in advance of release for them to host solely on their site for an agreed upon period of time (anywhere from 2 to 24 hours). It can be an excellent tool within a larger publicity strategy.

You cannot get a premiere if you have no exclusive content to offer. Ideal content for premieres includes an unreleased track, music video, or album. Note that other content (photos, lyric videos, behind the scenes extras) are not usually content that blogs have interest in premiering.

"I'm pretty averse to premieres in general, but that comes primarily from the blogger's perspective where managing those schedules tends to lead to more effort than it's worth. As an artist, a premiere can help give you a slight leg up as far as incentivizing someone to provide coverage. But beyond that, I'm not sure it's a huge draw these days. It's great to be able to share "victories" with your audience, but they're not going to care whether it was a premiere or not." **- Jason Grishkoff, Founder, SubmitHub & Indie Shuffle**

THE LOGISTICS OF SECURING A PREMIERE

Due to the fact that you are offering exclusive content, you should curate a list of 5-7 premiere targets. Once you have these ready and you are sure that they feature premieres, pitch each outlet one at a time.

It is bad form to offer two sites the same content simultaneously. You must wait to either hear back or feel like you've given the site enough time to respond, before reaching out to the next one. Start with your big goal sites and work your way down your list. I recommended waiting 4-7 days between pitches to give the blog ample time to respond. Pitch 2-3 times per blog then move onto the next. Submithub is a great resource for premiere pitching as they must respond to you in 24 hours.

Scoring a premiere on a major site is oftentimes not the end-all, be-all. The site that premiered your track may have a lot of prestige and a large following; however, your premiere will not be the main attraction on the site and may not even be on the homepage for a full 24 hours. With those stats in mind, it's easy to see the necessity for an effective social strategy coupled with additional features lined up after the premiere date.

"I came across an article in Rolling Stone, India and I took a note of the journalist's name. I reached out to him and sent him a link to my upcoming single. The result was surprisingly beautiful — they loved it and asked if they could premiere the song. It gave me a lot of confidence in reaching out to people myself and of not hiding behind my publicist. A lot of journalists and bloggers want to hear directly from the artist!" **- Rivita, Artist**

22
How To Rock Interviews

You have worked hard to pitch and follow up, and it has paid off! You have an invitation to do an interview. This is exciting, but it's also easy to blow this fantastic opportunity.

I have facilitated thousands of interviews over the years and have often received responses from clients that are, to be blunt, total crap. The reason for this is the artist didn't take the time to put thought and finesse into his responses and, frankly, one or two-word answers to any questions posed to you by a music writer make you look and sound like an arse.

In many cases, I won't even send poorly answered interviews back to editors because it makes my clients look bad.

I am often shocked when we get a lot of interviews for our artists and they start complaining about the fact that the media don't ask "interesting" questions, or they get the same question asked repeatedly.

Interviews are your opportunity to define your brand & control your narrative. Understand that any media interview poses a tremendous opportunity, even if the questions seem mundane, repetitive, or annoying, or the outlet is small.

The reason they are an opportunity is because people believe what others say about you more than they will ever believe what you say, and an interview in any publication is an endorsement from others where you drive the narrative. This is your chance to create responses that allow fans to go deeper with you as an artist.

But there's another reason to be prepared to put your best foot forward and crush your interview. That reason is Google. Your responses will be indexed by Google and searchable for years to come. In the future, when potential fans or industry folks want to know about you, they may very well search for articles. Strong interview responses are seeds for relationships you will be developing in your future that you don't even have yet.

CONVEY YOUR PERSONALITY, FEELINGS, AND VALUES

If you are dry-witted, silly, emotionally fragile, a hopeless romantic, or a rabble-rouser, you can show off your personality style in your responses. Interviews are also a place where you can communicate your feelings and values. These are probably most evident in your songwriting and recording style, and often they get lost in translation when it is time to express them on the written page. Show your vulnerability and create connections to themes and values in your music as they relate to you as a human being.

Not only is an email interview your opportunity to convey your style, but it's also one of your best opportunities to give potential fans a reason to hit play on that SoundCloud player or Spotify link that is most likely right there on the page as well. So, relatability is the key to get potential fans to listen to your music.

ALWAYS EXPAND UPON THE QUESTIONS

For instance, if you are asked "Who are you listening to these days?" A terrible answer is simply the name of the artist - for example "Blondie." This tells the reader absolutely nothing and does not give a why. Your job is to expand upon questions to make the responses more interesting and full of depth.

A better way to answer is: I recently saw Blondie live and it made me go back to their records from the '70s. It's amazing how they still stand up today production-wise and I admire Debbie Harry because she came up during a time when there were even fewer women in the music scene and she managed to become a fashion icon, a feminist voice, and she supported AIDS research and advocated for the LGBTQ+ community.

Here are two responses from a band and an artist from the blog Independent Artist Buzz. Notice how one artist, who shall remain nameless, took the easy way out and there's a typo (yes, most blogs won't spell check - that's also up to you!), and another artist expanded on her responses:

Q: Who are your musical inspirations; what artists inspired you to start your career and find your musical passion?

Oh I have so many! Inspirations... just a few... are James Taylor, Sara Bareilles, JP Saxe, Lennon Stella, Carole King, Ruston Kelly, I could keep going! I'm really inspired by other artists and how they tell their stories.

Look at this comparatively to Shelby Merchant's response:

Q: Who are your musical inspirations; what artists inspired you to start your career and find your musical passion?

Amy Winehouse is someone whose songwriting style influenced me from an early age. She's both blunt and tender in her imagery, and I like the sense of humor she brings to her lyrics. Carole King was also a big influence. Reading about her commercial approach to songwriting and how much time she spent writing every day gave me a sense of the reality of being a professional songwriter at a time when it seemed like an ephemeral dream. I also love her percussive approach to the piano.

Later in the interview Shelby expands on this and we can see why she resonates with Amy Winehouse, it all ties together.

Q: What is the most personal thing you have shared in your music or in your artist brand as it relates to being female?

I'm very open about my struggles with mental health. I have an anxiety disorder, and it's a pretty big thing for me. I've written about it before, in fact my next single "today was good" is about my method of dealing with it. Mental health affects men and women very differently, but isn't often treated as such. Two times more women attempt suicide than men. Mental health is terrible for anyone it affects, and I wish it was more commonly taught and talked about. In order to make progress with it we have to acknowledge that it treats different people differently.

Don't stray too far off topic. Expanding is good but straying wildly is not. It won't make sense for the flow of the interview. So be sure to stay on point.

One of the best ways to show that you are part of a tribe is to shine a light on others. When you're asked to give some musical comparisons or you are talking about your local scene, mention local venues and musicians that you know and already have established relationships with. Perhaps you can collaborate or play on the same bills. Mention artists who are within your reach to play gigs or tour with. Go the extra mile and hyperlink to those artist's tracks or websites, if appropriate. Then, when you share the article on socials after it is published, you can tag the venues and artists. It's possible that they will share your posts and their fans may take notice.

RESPECT WRITER'S DEADLINES

I can't tell you how many times this has happened, where we are hounding our clients to get us the responses for interviews we worked really hard to secure. I know you are busy, and sitting down to write responses may not feel natural to you. However, you're making your publicist look awful and you are showing the music writer that you don't respect them or their publication by not honoring deadlines. Trust me, the writer will remember that you were a pain in the ass to work with and, when the next opportunity to feature you arises, they may just go to one of the other 600 pitches in their inbox or go with an artist they know will respond punctually.

"Have a strong desire to meet deadlines and really do your best for the outlets that want to feature you. No feature is too small, and you should always feel gratitude for those that want to cover you, even if you and your publicist decide it's not a fit."
- Angela Mastrogiacomo, Owner, Muddy Paw PR

THOROUGHLY PROOFREAD YOUR INTERVIEW

It is not the blogger's or interviewer's job to proofread and correct any typos that you may have made. This does happen, of course (as does fact checking) at major newspapers and magazines who actually have copywriting staff on hand, but a music blog will not do this work for you. I advise you to show the article to a friend or two who have a keen eye for grammar, punctuation, and spelling and get their feedback.

If you are working with a music publicist, a good one will proof it for you but don't count on her to finesse your responses. You want her spending her time securing more features, not re-writing your responses.

THANK THE WRITER & SHARE

Thanking the writer who took the time to interview you in the first place is a gracious thing to do. Most musicians don't take this extra step and this is something you should always do, even if you have a publicist. Write a little note to the blogger at the end of the interview and include it in the text that you send to your publicist. If you are working with the writer directly, it's a classy touch to show gratitude. After the interview goes live, make sure to post on all of your socials and tag the publication and the writer, as well as other artists, venues, etc.

You (or your publicist) worked hard to land this interview. Now, it's time to share it. Not every publication shares every article that appears on their blog or site across their social channels, so the interview's visibility may depend solely on you. Visualize highlights using Canva or any other design app you like.

Share multiple ways and multiple times as assorted tweets and Instagram stories. And of course, create thoughtful, well-tagged Facebook & Instagram posts.

23
Live Show Publicity

Getting live show press is not easy. The main reason for this is the fact that there are fewer regional press outlets than there have ever been in the United States. When I had a traditional PR company in the '90s, I had over 12,000 newspapers alone in my database.

According to US News Deserts (www.usnewsdeserts.com), "At the end of 2019, the United States had 6,700 newspapers, down from almost 9,000 in 2004." And COVID-19 shuttered another 60 papers. Be prepared to be malleable around your expectations and placements if you are seeking live-show publicity.

"Every industry has been affected by the pandemic, and media and journalism are no exception. Many publications are hemorrhaging staff writers due to cuts, and these writers are moving to freelance positions and competing for the same opportunities. Staff are having to cover more stories, and with the added volume of music being released, they often don't have the bandwidth for premieres and emerging artist pitches. This, combined with fragmented attention, people juggling writing and editing and looking after kids at home. It's a lot!"
- Doug Hall, Founder, Big Feat PR

If you are lucky enough to have any live gigs booked and they are open to the public, start planning publicity for any dates 6-8 weeks before each show. You may have to be flexible, as many shows are getting shifted around quite regularly. As soon as a gig is booked, ask the promoter for the club's press list (most clubs have one). Promoters are dependent on this local press to help sell tickets.

CLUB LISTS AND VENUE PUBLICISTS

The club's press list is usually current and a great resource that will save you a lot of time, since you won't have to do all the research yourself. Ask the promoter who they think would be most likely to cover you as they know the local writers and tastemakers in their scenes better than you might, as those writers are probably hanging out in their bars or clubs regularly.

If the local promoter or club has an in-house publicist, ask to be connected to them. This publicist will also know the media and will be instrumental in helping you.

If the club does not have a press list, of course, you can easily search Google.

If you don't already have a profile on Bandsintown there may already be one waiting for you. This free site allows you to add all of your live shows (and many will get added automatically as they get their data from almost every venue and ticket seller imaginable). Fans who follow you on the platform are called trackers, and Bandsintown allows you to "post to trackers" for free to all of your followers to keep them up to date with new events, announcements or new music releases. To build followers on this platform, simply share your events landing page to your socials and in your newsletter. They also have a cool feature that allows you to geo-target your trackers, so if you are playing a specific market you can alert only fans in that area about that show. Since the pandemic, Bandsintown also allows you to post all of your livestreaming events so add those as well.

The first few times you play a market, you may not get any press. If you are new and worried because you didn't get covered the first time around, keep sending information every time you play in the area. I have never met a writer who ignores several pitches from the same band sent over and over again. It may take a few tours through each market, but the more a writer sees you over time, the more likely he or she is to write about you.

24
Getting On Spotify Playlists

There are 3 types of playlists - **editorial, personalized**, and **listener**. It is crucial to understand the differences among them.

Editorial - These are the playlists that are curated by Spotify's staff and by algorithms (you don't actually think that Spotify has enough staff to listen to the tens of thousands of submissions, do you?) These are the playlists with the little Spotify logo in the top-left corner of the cover image.

HOW TO GET ON EDITORIAL (OFFICIAL SPOTIFY) PLAYLISTS

In order to get on Spotify curated playlists you need to submit your track directly to Spotify for consideration. Go to artists.spotify.com then choose the song you'd like to send to Spotify's curation team for review. Fill out the description for your track fully. The more information and detail you provide, the better your chances are for getting picked up. I will go over how to get on non-curator playlists later in this guide.

You have 500 characters to use for your Playlist Submission. Take the time to think through a solid pitch and use as close to 500 as you can. During the submission process, you will also get to tag your song correctly for mood, genre, instruments used, etc. to make sure that Spotify delivers it to more listeners that are likely to engage. Metadata is key.

"We always tell artists and their teams to submit as early as possible, but a very last minute submission resulted in editorial playlist features. We recommend putting as much cred as possible in the submission. What is there in your story, or about you as an artist, that is unique or powerful that can give you credibility? For example, did you open for Post Malone on tour, or did Ariana Grande sing background vocals on your track? Make a list of your best cred and then use it in the pitch. You are looking to get the editors to click on the link to your music , and giving them enough info so that they want to dig further. Whatever you can say that can help that along is your goal. You only have 500 characters to get the job done on Spotify. We really work to craft these submissions, and suggest that you and your team spend some time thinking about what data points you can include that can help get attention for your music. Describe the music, your path as an artist, collaborations, tours, marketing, and other key components of your career.

Here are 2 submissions where the track ended up being featured on Spotify editorial playlists, but we'd be the last to say that its our submission that did it, it's more about the music and what the curator is looking for at that moment, and hopefully the submission helps them move to listen and / or feature it!

Example #1

XXXXXX XXXXXXXX is a country singer songwriter who brings a pop touch to her soulful sound. She's an LA girl now, but she attributes her country background to growing up in Arizona. She's recorded 2 CDs in Nashville, and is now working on a new EP in LA that's being produced by Avi Kaplan, formerly of Pentatonix. She's opened for Chris Bandi at Caesar's Vegas, Toby Keith at Coastal Country Jam in Cali, Bebe Rexha at Phoenix Pride, Ashley Monroe at The Hotel Cafe, and Jason Aldean at CountryFest.

Example #2

Known for his theme and music for one of YouTube's biggest channels, "XXXXXXXX," XXXXX XXXXXXXX has had 7 different #1 spots on the Hype Machine Top 50, and his music is some of the most used on podcast themes and outtros. His chillwave hiphop beats, electronic sound, and 'unpredictable percussive adds' have him likened to Tycho, Flying Lotus, Toro y Moi."
- Andrea Young, Founder and Partner of DPG Worldwide

Artists spend an inordinate amount of time and energy focused on landing on editorial playlists, as they are the most prominent. They are also the hardest to get on. Just like with publicity on blogs, start small and build up on your path to the larger inclusions.

Personalized - These playlists are algorithmically generated for all users on the Spotify platform. They include Discover Weekly and Release Radar, and they are unique for each listener, based on their unique tastes and preferences. Spotify also creates seasonal personalized playlists like Wrapped and Summer Rewind. These are generated by algorithms.

HOW TO GET ON PERSONALIZED (RELEASE RADAR) PLAYLISTS

All Spotify users get customized weekly Release Radar playlist curated for them on Fridays, and any of your friends and fans who pre-save your music or heart your profile will automatically receive your new tracks on the day your music comes out. Release Radar is one of the key reasons artists should be getting as many fans as possible to pre-save and follow their profiles on Spotify.

Release Radar playlists are algorithmic, meaning the more plays that you generate the better your chances of Spotify's algorithms picking up on you. which, in turn, will add you to more playlists. Eventually, you may get the most desired tier of playlists — the Spotify curated lists — which have the most visibility and followers on the platform.

> *"The more followers [you have], the more Release Radar playlists you go into...What we are seeing is that this playlist is becoming a huge driver of streams – more than any of our programmed editorial playlists, which are the ones that everyone pitches for. It's Release Radar which is driving listens."*
> **- Bryan Johnson, Head of Industry Partnerships, Spotify UK**

Your non-musician friends probably don't understand why it's important that they follow you, so explain the value to them. Fans love to help and often they don't know how to do so, so being honest about the how and why behind things you'd like them to do is crucial.

RUN A PRE-SAVE CAMPAIGN

Pre-save links allow your fans to save your songs on their favorite streaming platform before you release. On release day, your fans will get a notification that your music is out and it will be added to their Release Radar playlist.

You must use a third party to create a pre-save link. I suggest choosing from these two platforms:

Show.co - If you have a CD Baby account, you should go with Show.co, as it is free for certain customers. Once your release is approved, all you need is your CD Baby UPC code to set up the pre-save. The set-up process will require things like your release date and album artwork.

Feature.fm – A great solution if you use any other distributor, as they provide great looking links and tools for marketing.

You can also gather email addresses through both of these marketing platforms and I suggest you do.

ASK SPECIFICALLY FOR SPOTIFY FOLLOWERS ON YOUR SOCIALS

Your Spotify account should be connected to all of your socials.

- Post on Facebook (and BOOST!). If you use your personal profile for your music, DM people and ask for follows
- Create a post on Instagram and change your bio link for a few days or add to your linktr.ee – message individually and share
- Create an Instagram story and ask
- Include a call-to-action (CTA) on your videos asking people to come save your profile or tracks. Post on Instagram, Twitter, and Facebook
- Make a graphic for Twitter asking to follow you – also use DM
- Post a short ask on your blog (if you have one)
- Ask in your monthly email as a CTA

SEND A DEDICATED SPOTIFY EMAIL

Email your list and make "come follow me on Spotify" your CTA

This is also a good time to send personal emails to friends and family who are not on your list. It may be time-consuming but it's a great way to get people onto your list who you may not have asked already. Plus, this is such a simple ask and it only takes a few seconds for your friends to do.

INCLUDE A FOLLOW BUTTON ON YOUR WEBSITE

I know you want to lead people straight to your iTunes store to buy the music, but the truth is they probably won't do this. Why? Because they use Spotify!

So, a Spotify follow button is a good addition to your socials as many people will prefer to stream your music.

SHARE COLLABORATIVE PLAYLISTS

Create playlists with similar music to yours, so that when fans check them out they are more likely to follow you because you have a similar sound. By connecting yourself with other artists of your type, and pushing this out to the world, you can begin to create a fanbase that appreciates your taste in music.

Listener - These playlists are made by users. There are millions of them, and you can and should make some to share with your fans. Curate by theme or genre or mood and add a few of your own tracks.

HOW TO GET ON LISTENER PLAYLISTS

Listener playlists have anywhere from dozens of engaged followers to millions. And a little elbow grease and smart communication will land you on these lists. Listener playlists can carry huge influence and potential for your music.

Note: You must have a paid, premium account to do this.

Login to Spotify and search for a band or an artist who is slightly larger than you — maybe one to two years ahead of where you are right now. Choose an artist you have played with or who you know would have the same fans. Locate the "About" section of that artist's profile.

You will see, on the right-hand side, a list of all of the playlists on which they've been included. It will appear under the heading "Discovered On." Next, click on each playlist and look at the Spotify user who created the playlist under "Created By" and see if you can find a first and last name. Next, search for the person on Facebook (look for individual people, pages). In many cases, Facebook and Spotify are connected because people login to Spotify using their Facebook accounts.

After you have found a human curator send them a message and add them as a friend so that the message goes to Facebook Messenger and not in the dreaded "other" box. On Messenger, explain that you found their playlist on Spotify.

Get personal here — say something you specifically like about their playlist, and then request that they listen to your track because you think it will fit in! Don't skip this step and just send a cut and pasted email. Make this part of the process personal and it will pay off.

Also, find the playlister on Instagram and send a DM there as well.

You will need to do this many times before you will get any traction. Doing it only a few times might not yield any results, but your consistency and volume will pay off (go for 25 as your target like you did with blogs and media).

"Here's what I tell people who ask me how to write a solid pitch: make me feel like I have listened to your song in less than 2 paragraphs. If you aren't good with words, find someone who is. Hand them a pen and paper, then play the song to them and ask them to write about it. You may need to try this with a few people to find something that aligns best with how you want your song to be represented. If you are a producer and collaborate with a singer / songwriter, they are already good with words... ask them to attempt writing the pitch first before asking others. If you are independent, don't mention your marketing budget (unless you have one). If you are established and investing significant money in promoting your release through social media, billboards etc. then definitely include this at the end of your pitch." - **Mike Warner, Author, *Work Hard Playlist Hard***

PART 5
Intentional Publicity

H ere's the reality: There are hundreds of thousands of artists that fall into the category of "Record, release, record, release, repeat, repeat..." There's nothing wrong with this, but there's another way of approaching your career that will open up a whole world of publicity and other opportunities and allow you to not only make music but also travel the world as Maya Azucena does, help the elderly as Ilyana Kadushin does, or bring important causes to light as Michelle Shocked does. I call this intentional publicity.

Intentional publicity does not mean that you do something inauthentic to who you are. This will never work, and the media and fans will see right through you. But it does include aligning your vision and actions with causes, social justice or building a community around specific themes as Heather Mae has done.

There are many forms of intentional publicity, and musicians who have chosen this path or stumbled into it reap the benefits of getting more exposure in the media because they are more newsworthy.

25
Cause-Related Publicity

Cause-related publicity comes when musicians pair their art with causes and missions that they are truly passionate about. You can create income streams from those passions using platforms like Patreon. There are many benefits to operating like this but the one I want to point out is this: when you embrace causes larger than yourself, you become NEWSWORTHY. You become your own publicity machine. All of a sudden, entire niche markets open up that have their own blogs, radio shows, and podcasts associated with whatever it is you choose to embrace.

Cause-related artists can't help but add their social justice, charities, and platforms into the mix. Ilyana Kadushin brilliantly calls this having a "multi-hyphenated mixed career." I have followed Ilyana's career since I publicized her first album in 2004 and I have watched with wonder as she has grown and expanded her career over the years. The most impressive part is how she blends her activism into every facet of her career.

ARTIST HIGHLIGHT:

ILYANA KADUSHIN
The Alchemy Of Art Meeting Activism

Instagram: @ilyanakadushin

I have always been curious about the ways I could engage myself creatively. I became one of those "multi-hyphenated mixed career" identities and over the years I transformed what this meant to me.

Some of us may do the multi-hyphenated career out of financial necessity and some may choose this kind of career path because it feeds us on every level. At my core I am a storyteller, and every kind of work I do is some form of connecting with an audience, telling a story and using my voice and platforms to do so. Along my path, my artist side met my activist side and they have been married ever since. And I think there's an alchemy to this kind of marriage. I love being an artist and a performer, and yes we all need to be entertained and have our imaginations delighted and sparked by art! But at some point I realized I needed to engage what I did creatively with the community at large and in ways that would also meet a need in these communities. The lens that I started to look through in all my work was "being of service." The world needs artists to inspire, challenge, and transform us. Let's get back to that word, Alchemy, a seemingly magical process of transformation, creation, or combination. Despite the fact that this multi-hyphenate way of working can be incredibly challenging and requires a ton of focus and energy, the outcomes I experienced from these projects were magical. As you will see in my "career trajectory" that I have included, opportunities for my art to meet activism kept arriving and I seized them!

As a performer I have worked in documentary theater pieces that collaborated with companies that include: Amnesty International Human Rights Week: Anti-Trafficking Initiatives, True Body Project: about empowering women and girls; and Birth Project: examining women's birth rights. I have performed in music concerts for Vday, Wildlife Federation, and Rock & Renew.

As a voice performer and singer for film, television, and multimedia, I worked with companies that included: Nickelodeon, Sesame Street, BBC America, and Cartoon Network. My voice-over work spans numerous national commercials, animation, and video games — my fave? Lord of The Rings! My narration credits include, Star Wars, Dune, and the bestselling Twilight series. And then, as a voice performer, my art met activism when I narrated Nadia Murad's memoir called The Last Girl; about a Yazidi human rights activist from Iraq, who won the Nobel Peace Prize in 2018. Telling Nadia's incredible story to American audiences was so moving.

As a singer and co-producer, I collaborate with my husband, James Harrell, a composer and producer. We co-produce and perform music that is heard in commercials and films, including Hunters on Amazon Prime, and the soundtrack of a 2011 HBO award-winning documentary film called Separate, But Equal. My art met activism in this arena, when I started touring colleges and spoke about creating this film with the director, Shawn Wilson. We led town hall conversations with students on race and community esteem that revealed our shared humanity.

James and I I co-host and produce a podcast called No, I Know, where I interview people making a difference in their communities; like Daryl Davis (Musician and Author of Klandestine Relationships) and Reverend Pat Bumgardner, (leader at MC church which is inclusive for the LGBTQ communities) and we play live music on the podcast as well.

As an educator, I am adjunct faculty at my alma mater, NYU Tisch School of The Arts, teaching upper-level voice and public speaking. I felt a great need to assist future generations in being able to communicate better with their audiences, about their work, and themselves in effective and powerful ways.

In 2017, I founded my own nonprofit, Stories Love Music, which provides a free, creative engagement program for caregivers who care for senior citizens. I decided to start this non-profit after hurricane Sandy, when I realized that both our senior citizens and their caregivers were facing isolation, depression, and burnout and that receiving creative engagement like music and storytelling, was vital to the meaning and health of their lives.

There are many times when I get overwhelmed in the face of the huge issues that I am addressing in my work, so I will take a beat and remind myself why I do this kind of work. I realized that the way I think about my work creates an energy around it and this energy can either be limiting or expansive. It is also imperative that you are an advocate for yourself and make sure there is reciprocity in all your work. All the parts of my career are inter-connected and when I approach them this way, it is more energizing and contributes to the magic they can offer the world.

I first heard Maya Azucena's incredible voice in 2004 when she was a featured vocalist on Pete Miser's album, and I was mesmerized. Then I met her and realized she was one of the coolest and kindest artists I had ever come across, and she has a special way of putting you at ease and connecting with everyone she meets in a way that makes them feel like they are the only person in the room. It is no mystery that she became an in-demand performer at countless benefits and she makes the world her living room.

ARTIST HIGHLIGHT:

MAYA AZUCENA
Building International Appeal As Humanitarian, Advocate, And Indie Artist

Instagram @mayaazucena

Brooklyn-born, critically acclaimed, avid independent global touring artist and songwriter, Maya Azucena, is well known for her humanitarian outlook and projects around the world, which include special focuses on women's and youth empowerment and domestic/sexual violence. Based on a personal commitment to help the world through her talent, most of Maya's songs are anthems that lend a voice to self-worth, empowerment, overcoming obstacles, and stepping into our "fearless" selves. Here is Maya's story:

Fellow artists ask me how it is that I travel the world so frequently and to such diverse locations. Inside of my responses, I try to explain that there is more to our opportunities than what the mainstream entertainment industry platforms offer. There is also more opportunity when we learn that the world is the market – not just the country or city we live in.

From a grassroots perspective, I retrained my mind to see avenues available to me outside of the obvious and highly limited choices that the industry offers. What happens if you're not signed to a solid record deal, or if you have less than 200K followers on YouTube, or if you don't have $30,000+ to get one song played on radio? What you can do is remember that there are 8 billion people on this planet and most of them like music! Target audience? Them!

When I had the epiphany that "music is my calling," I started to consciously apply my talent to help the world around me. I feverishly wrote songs with substance, about my observations of injustice, about my own tales of survival, about never giving up, about reclaiming our power, trusting our inner beauty, and about the ever-present hope that waits for us all. These subjects inside my songs combined nicely with the decision to lend my voice to almost any charity or social justice event I could find in New York City. I landed many things that address women and girl's empowerment. I gravitated to these particularly, as a result of my past experience inside a violent relationship.

Inevitably, I was that artist people knew to call when there was a benefit or cause. I had successfully begun to brand myself for something unusual – which means I was one of the few who got the call for paid work in this fringe market. Guess what? There is a broad base of humanitarians and social activists all around the world. They create conferences and conventions, retreats, and festivals. Most of these people, thousands and thousands of them, are not even in the music industry!

I started in small but passionate events in NYC, and ultimately ended up receiving awards and being invited to things nationally and globally. I was on Washington D.C.'s National Mall in front of 10,000 people, singing my song "Warriors" during a Save Darfur gathering. I spoke and did a concert for TedxWomen at the International Institute of Peace. I performed at Omega Institute for 400 international women leaders, from many countries, who came to share their efforts for social change and buoy each other's initiatives. I've spoken and sung to 1,000 female students at University New Delhi, India, about domestic violence and how to activate sustainable change. I've spoken to dignitaries and feminist activists, as keynote speaker, in Dar Es Salaam Tanzania, on the subject of Art and its contribution to the fight for women's rights. I performed a concert at Women Deliver, a conference on maternal health. Honduras. Kingdom of Lesotho. Haiti. Suriname. Croatia. Turkey. Philippines, a dozen more. These things came to me because I did not wait for the music industry to "accept" me. I mean, I do mainstream clubs and festivals too! I've toured all over Europe and done SXSW in Austin, Texas four times. But, I found that if I limit myself only to the narrative of being "discovered" and "sponsored" into a mainstream heaven of pop success, then I would not have survived all these years. My grassroots, bumpy, off-the-beaten-path journey has actually paid my bills and given me a strong foundation, and respect, as an independent artist. In other words, I have an active career, rather than a pipe dream.

I was glad to see that we artists have access to millions of people, outside the box, when we think...outside the box.

For anyone who listened to music in the '90s, the name Michelle Shocked will be very familiar. She was gracious enough to heed my callout for inspiring ways that musicians have grown their tribes and expanded upon their visions, and her tale of Roadworks is a great one to model for when the world opens up again (or to create now, virtually). Michelle's bio is in the first person like Heather Mae's and I'm not gonna touch it because it's fantastic.

This could be easily replicated in a livestreaming format for today's COVID-19 age of fan building. I did quite a bit of Googling for Roadworks and Michelle Shocked and unsurprisingly, there was a ton of press around these live events. It fits the bill on so many levels because it shines the light on others (the special guests), it raises awareness for charities and social justice issues which are very close to her heart, and it gave fans a chance to hear the favorites they loved for years with new artists and special guests added to the mix. She brought her tribe along for the ride.

ARTIST HIGHLIGHT:

MICHELLE SHOCKED
*The Creation Of Roadworks, A Seasonal Circuit, And A
Template For A Touring Subscription Model*

Instagram @mshockedrox

Thirty four years into a career with complete ownership of an amazing, critically-acclaimed, internationally-recognized catalog, and I have managed to extricate myself from the biggest bootleg operation the world has ever seen. I've paid a high price, certainly. I'll continue to search for alternatives where creative control and artistic integrity might be practiced beyond our digital dystopia. The current degree of DMCA dysfunction offers little light at the end of a very long tunnel, either for new or legacy artists. The .01% of artists who receive 90% of the streaming revenue may be the names you'll recall. But for the 99% of us dying at a rate of extinction faster than the Amazon tree frog, the songs we wrote that you never heard will be all that remains of our story.

And here's what Michelle sent me:

I am a legacy singer-songwriter who pioneered the genre of Americana in the early 90s. For five years, I developed a proof of concept I called Roadworks which traveled seasonally, following the moderate weather, successfully creating a template for a touring subscription model.

Each year of my five-year project had a theme. In the first year, it was around a new release called "Soul of My Soul." The second and third year, however, were for catalog reissues celebrating anniversary milestones. The fourth year was a grassroots political organizing effort, called "Roccupy, supporting homeowners fighting against foreclosure fraud by the banks," inspired by the

Occupy Wall Street uprising.

The format for these shows were divided into three parts; the first was a presentation of the feature material for that year's theme, the second part was a spotlight on a local act or organizer, and the third part was a closing segment of fan favorites and requests, often with special guests sitting in.

Although the timing of Roadworks was slightly prior to the datafication that would define metrics-based marketing soon thereafter, the concept of touring seasonally still holds true. Spring months - March, April and May - traveled from the Southwest to the Northwest to the Midwest. Fall months - September, October, November - traveled from the Northeast to the UK to the Southeast. Between ten and twelve shows in each of these months allowed me to budget cost-effectively and have a healthy, balanced period of time at home to rest and create...recreate!

The audiences were satisfied with a touring rhythm that gave them an expectation of when I would next be coming through town each year.

To address the challenge of underfunded marketing for new releases, the Roadworks project was designed as an elaborate teaser campaign for my as-yet-unreleased masterwork, Indelible Women.

What we can learn here is that combining issues that Michelle was deeply passionate about with a smart and episodic approach really made an impact. The format is amazing:

Part 1: A presentation of the feature material for that year's theme

Part 2: A spotlight on a local act or organizer

Part 3: A closing segment of fan favorites and requests, often with special guests sitting in

There are countless examples of artists who have become thought leaders around causes, like Amanda Palmer who created one of the most inspiring TED talks you could ever watch about artists and their muses, and the art of asking: and Blake Morgan, who is an activist who fights for musician's rights (look up his Wikipedia then send him a thank-you note for fighting for you in the halls of Congress).

26
Niche-Based Publicity

Your angle does not have to be based in social justice or charities. With 30 million blogs out there to connect with, your niche could be anything you want. The more "niche" you can get, the more you will become known in that niche, and the more success you'll have not only with publicity but also with overall career success. I have observed over the years that artist tend to want everyone to like them , but the truth is you don't need everyone to like you to create a sustainable career. You only need a small, focused niche.

A niche is not "travel." Instead, it's "European backpacking," or "shamanistic journey." Get granular within your niche. We've run entire content marketing and publicity campaigns around this concept.

One artist who sprung to mind immediately as one who's nailed a niche is Michelle Citrin. Here is an excerpt from her bio:

MICHELLE CITRIN - "THE JEWISH IT GIRL"

At just 5'1", it's hard to believe that such a powerful voice could come out of Michelle Citrin. There is a reason why Time.com recently listed Michelle in their Top Ten list of "New Jewish Rock Stars" and the Jerusalem Post calls Michelle "The Jewish It Girl."

Michelle is best known as the creator and star of viral video hits including "20 Things to do with Matzah," "Call Your Zeyde", "Rosh Hashanah Girl" and "Hanukkah Lovin." In total, these videos have received millions of hits from around the world and have led to the press referring to Michelle as, "a YouTube sensation."

Michelle's viral video successes have led to media coverage ranging from the New York Times to the Huffington Post as well as Good Morning America, CNN, CBS and even being featured on Yahoo.com's homepage. This year, Michelle had the great honor of performing the National Anthem and her original soulful pop-folk in front of a crowd of 13,000 people including members of Congress.

Fully independent from any record label, Michelle has sold thousands of copies of her albums. Her engaging live performances and talent for writing catchy and meaningful songs have garnered rave reviews and numerous accolades, including being named one of Billboard Music's "Top Songwriters," VH-1's Song of the Year finalist, a Great American Songwriting Honor, and finalist in Sony Music's Future Rock Competition.

You can add any of these niches on top of your primary platform, and that's the beauty of this strategy. You definitely want to get thinking about what resonates with you — what are you passionate about? There, you'll find your niche.

RACHAEL SAGE - CREATED AN INSPIRATIONAL TRIBUTE TO SURVIVORSHIP

Rachael is an indie artist who has had a long, successful career. A few years ago, Rachael battled cancer, and, as a survivor, she has shared her experience through her art, as well as created a series of fundraisers to benefit women's cancer awareness. Of course, being a cancer survivor is not her only niche but it is something she has shared, and it has become one of her many niches. She is also an ex-ballerina, the owner of an indie record label that releases other female artists, a painter, and has raised money for many causes throughout the years, including hurricane relief. Here's her bio:

Since founding her own label, MPress Records, two decades ago, NYC-based alt-pop artist Rachael Sage has steadily released a slew of vibrant, dynamic albums with poetic lyrics spanning subjects as wide as her inspirations. She has toured with an eclectic list of artists including Ani DiFranco, Beth Hart, Sarah McLachlan, Judy Collins, and Howard Jones. Sage also continues to significantly grow her visibility via her many song placements, including 22 songs on top reality show Dance Moms, translating into over 10 million YouTube hits. Her latest single and video, "Blue Sky Days," was originally composed as a meditation on gratitude in the midst of her own recent cancer recovery, but has taken on new resonance during COVID-19. Sage's new album "Character" is an inspirational tribute to survivorship. The collection reflects on such concepts as identity, compassion, authenticity, optimism, and mindfulness. As Sage confesses, "I don't think I understood the full meaning of the word 'character' until I was suddenly required to redefine my own...if there is a silver-lining in all of this, it's that I have a much deeper relationship to gratitude."

For Sage, survivorship now means balancing her new commitment to staying healthy with a renewed sense of purpose: creating work that uplifts and empowers others in any way she possibly can. The former ballerina says she has "come to realize that music is the most powerful healing tool I have ever encountered. It has quite literally saved my life, and I intend for the rest of my career to be a long, slow dance of gratitude."

As a fierce advocate for girls and women, Beth Kille has managed to carve out her niche based on community by inspiring creativity in others.

ARTIST HIGHLIGHT:

BETH KILLE OF GIN, CHOCOLATE, & BOTTLE ROCKETS
We All Sink Or Swim Together

Instagram: @bethkille

Beth Kille is a 22-time Madison Area Music Association (MAMA) award-winning artist from Madison, WI, who has been cranking out Americana Rock tunes since 2000. Her stage prowess was recognized in 2011 when she received Artist of the Year honors at the Madison Area Music Awards – a rare accomplishment for a solo artist. Beth also works as an audio engineer / producer, songwriting instructor, the Executive Producer of the Madison Area Music Association Awards, the host of Madison's Sing It Sister Showcase, the Music Director for Girls & Ladies Rock Camp Madison, and most importantly, as a mom. Her mission in life is to inspire all to embrace their creativity. Her band Gin, Chocolate & Bottle Rockets is composed of business partners who are also inseparable friends. They have discovered the three components of perfect harmony, and they teach how to implement them by creating a one-hour, Living in Harmony presentation. In it, they share three key components to help compose a life you love. They have presented for numerous organizations and schools including American Family Dreambank, The University of Wisconsin School of Medicine, Divine Savior HealthCare System and the Brava Women's Expo.

From Beth:

My mantra for local musicians is "We all sink or swim together," meaning, if we don't support each other on the local scene and lift one another up, our local scene is doomed for failure.

I fronted a rock band in Madison, WI, called Clear Blue Betty from 2002-2008. We enjoyed a fair amount of success on the local scene, winning several local and regional awards and playing some of the city's more prestigious events. I was working a day job as a physical therapist at that time but was gigging as much as possible on the weekends. In 2008 my husband, who conveniently doubled as my drummer, had the opportunity to do one year of job training in Houston, TX, so the band dissolved when we moved. I took a giant leap and quit my day job at that time. I figured, since it was a short stint in a new town and I wasn't licensed to practice in Texas I might as well take the plunge.

While in Texas, I met an amazing musical mentor by the name of Connie Mims. I lovingly dubbed her the "Rockin' Fairy Godmother of the Houston Music Scene." It seemed she had a passion and knack for creating opportunities for other artists to create and share their music. I was so inspired by Connie that I decided when we returned to Madison, I was going to try to do the same.

When we moved back to Madison, I banded together with other local musicians to help develop a Girls Rock Camp — a summer day camp for girls ages 8-18. Our first year of camp was in 2010. We held one camp with 32 girls. Due to its popularity, we expanded to three separate weeks of camp with 150 kids over the course of the summer. I also ran an open mic for a bit, served as the coordinator for Madison's chapter of the Nashville Songwriters Association International for a couple years, developed a quarterly showcase for local female singers to play with a house band (Sing it Sister), co-founded an annual music festival called Flannel Fest, created my own home studio where I record albums for emerging artists, joined the volunteers of the Madison Area Music Association, and eventually took over as the Executive Producer of their annual Grammy-style awards show.

I also currently play in three different bands where I have the joy of collaborating with brilliant and talented local musicians. My trio, with Shawndell Marks and Jen Farley, called Gin, Chocolate & Bottle Rockets, recently embarked on a motivational speaking side gig. Our signature talk is "Living in Harmony" where we discuss the importance of sharing a common mission, the beauty of partnering with people who have different styles, and the importance of staying in the moment to achieve harmony in life.

So, long story short, I went a little overboard.

Now, in case you think I'm some kind of android working 24-7, let me tell you, I am most definitely not. Do I work extremely hard and love what I do? Absolutely. But I have a kid, a husband, a dog, I eat pretty healthy, exercise regularly, and have a bit of a life outside of the music scene. Here's the key: I did all of these things in partnership with outstanding people over the past 11 years. And as a result, we have all been able to SWIM together in the music scene.

Girls Rock Camp is a prime example. This program has had tremendous impact on the women in this community - myself included - in that we all support and lift each other. The women who work for this camp share gigs, play on each other's albums, gain year-round students for their private music lesson studios, and find access to wider audiences in their performances. We give of ourselves to teach kids about music, collaboration, and empowerment, and we get back ten-fold from the campers, their families, and the community.

There have been plenty of bumps and hiccups along the way but it has been a joy and privilege to work with so many dedicated people who understand the importance of community in music. There is something special about our music scene. It doesn't feel cut-throat or competitive to me. I believe any community can create this kind of fertile ground for it's musicians. It just takes teamwork.

27
Crowdfunding Publicity

Another category of intentional publicity is the type you can generate for your crowdfunding campaign. Many artists ask me how to get publicity for their crowdfunding or Patreon campaigns, believing that if they can get PR traction around their fundraising efforts it will result in more contributions.

If your campaign is doing something that can potentially make a huge impact for a local community (for example, charity work, raising money to save a school, local theater, or an animal shelter), or if your campaign is totally quirky or original and "newsworthy," then publicity might be worth exploring. If you can't get any blogs or podcasts on board you can always spin your own publicity wheels by writing for "submit your story" blogs .

Any publicity that you generate should be specifically focused on the niches that fit your campaign. For example, one of my clients ran a crowdfunding campaign to raise money to create and launch a finger-picking guitar course. Therefore, she sought publicity from blogs and podcasts that focus on guitar teachers and on the art of guitar playing, and she managed to land several placements that tied in her guitar playing and teaching expertise with her crowdfunding campaign.

Come up with at least 3-5 additional niches to increase your chances of success. Niche examples aside from music include technology, fashion, travel, health and wellness, book reviews, cooking, and parenting. Of course, these have to pertain to your crowdfunding campaign. You can drill down even further here and identify niches that focus your outreach even more. Some cases of more specific niches might be mobile technology, affordable fashion, and singles travel.

Creating great content that is not only about your campaign but is also beneficial to the blog or podcast's community is key. For my own crowdfunding campaign, I approached each blogger personally via email explaining that I was launching a crowdfunding campaign and I would appreciate it if they could share what I had to say with their own followers and readers. I took these opportunities to share some of my overall music marketing knowledge with each blogger. Then, I mentioned the crowdfunding campaign at the end, as part of the conversation so it didn't look like a giant advertisement for my crowdfunding campaign. It turned into a feature with a mention.

BEWARE OF CROWDFUNDING PR PACKAGES

There are many crowdfunding public relations and promotion firms promoting their "crowdfunding PR packages" online. Many artists have contacted me saying "I put my campaign up on Kickstarter and this PR firm contacted me the very next day!" That's because firms like these troll crowdfunding sites and when they see a new project launch they reach out to offer services. I once interviewed a programmer who was often hired by firms to write code to trigger these types of outreach emails automatically, but sadly most don't realize they are part of a mass email phishing campaign and their egos make expensive decisions. I caution against hiring a PR firm to help you handle your crowdfunding unless you get a clear vision from them with specific targets for exactly where they will seek to get publicity for you, and what their reasons are for believing you will actually get placements in the press.

28
In Real Life (IRL) Publicity

There's a publicity world which happens on the other side of the computer and many musicians don't take to it easily. It's known as IRL PR, or to be as blunt as I can: networking. Artists who have mastered the art of IRL PR are walking talking PR machines. Amanda Palmer is a quintessential example.

Connecting the dots of your digital world to the real world is a crucial part of moving forward, not only for PR but also for your music career. Even if you only want to be a studio musician or license your music and have no interest in playing live gigs or touring, you still need to be able to meet people to network with and discover potential future work. It can be hard to break out of your comfort zone, and I have met many artists who struggle with anxiety and have a notion that networking means "selling" or being cheesy. The most successful musicians are those who go out and meet other people who can help them.

There's a problem with all of the digital tools available to us: Way too many artists are hiding behind screens and trying to launch careers of their dreams without connecting with others face-to-face. PR in real life is critical and will get you far if you know how to do it effectively.

"Get to know the people who can help you out. Faces and conversations are easier to remember than emails and press releases. Obviously that only works on a local level, but the principle is the same. Maybe get involved in their projects,

contribute to their podcast, turn up at the shows they are involved in, write a guest blog for their site, whatever it may be that moves you from the "another muso" corner to the "friends and acquaintances" pile. There are millions of people looking for the same break as you but people are much more likely to help out a friend. When I was mainly a live gig booker, I used to get loads of bands sending emails and links in an attempt to get a gig, more than I was prepared to listen to in a day. It's just the way it is. One day I had a message from a guy in a band who said, I'm going to be in your part of town today. Do you fancy meeting for lunch? So I met with him, we found out we had a lot in common, had a great conversation and ended up becoming good friends. After that first meeting, when the band name came up they were no longer just anonymous musicians on a list but seemed more human and obviously got slightly preferential consideration." **- Dave Franklin, Editor, Dancing About Architecture & Freelance Music Journalist**

There are 3 reasons musicians need to master IRL PR: To gain new fans and connect with current ones, to gain a sphere of influence in the business and a source for referrals (more fans, more gigs, etc.), and to become a resource for anyone who meets you.

Pre COVID-19 you were probably in social situations often, and for the sake of this section of the book pretend that it's 2019 again – gigs, parties, work events, picking your kids up at school, the grocery store, etc. These can all become networking opportunities to connect with potential fans.

Here are some real-life IRL PR 101 tips that I learned from Larry Sharpe, who is a business consultant, entrepreneur, and internet broadcaster. Larry is such a master at networking that people literally line up to talk to him at events. I know this because the day I met him, I stood in line to do so.

If you truly want to grow your fan community through networking, your biggest goal when you go out is: be memorable. How do you do that? Simple: The more they talk, the more memorable you are.

This is not about being sales-like. It's just a mindset. Many artists who have mastered this mindset are featured throughout this book. Everywhere they go, they amass fans and opportunities for themselves because they present an opportunity for others to want to connect with them.

Here are some tips for even the biggest introverts.

When you meet someone new, start by asking a question about them. "What brought you here today?" "How did you meet the band that you opened for tonight?" Get them talking. You will be amazed at how quickly they'll jump in, it takes the pressure of talking about yourself off of you.

When it's time to introduce yourself, never start out with the typical greeting of "Hi my name is...." That makes it all about you. Instead, you want to say something like, "So, what do you do?" Or, "Are you having a good time?" Or, "What brings you here today?" Or "Aren't these mini donuts amazing?" Now, it's all about them and how their experience is going.

Once you get them talking and they are beginning to open up, see how you can help them. Do they want information? Tips on something specific? Music lessons for their kid? The best bakery in town for red velvet cupcakes? A great place to buy an outfit? A car mechanic? You know, stuff. Is there anything you could possibly share that you know to help them?

What you may find as you are being helpful is they may naturally, in turn, ask how they can be helpful to you. Then it's your turn to make a request. If you do not have a specific goal that day, getting a social media connection is always a way to naturally expand your online reach.

After they have talked about themselves and they ask you about your music, a great way to introduce your music is to mention what other people say about you, instead of pitching yourself from your point of view.

Why? Because people always believe what other people say about you more than they believe what you say about yourself.

So, you could say something like: "People say my music sounds like_____with a touch of _____." Or, "My voice gets compared to _____." This will register in a way that, again, takes the focus off of you and it may feel a lot more comfortable.

Being a Gatherer is the key here. This means that whenever you are in any social situation, you should be gathering as much information as possible about each person: interesting tidbits, what they like, who they know, where they go, etc. This way you can help them! Make a list on your phone after a conversation to make sure you don't forget any.

THE ART OF THE FOLLOW-UP

When it comes time to follow up, don't send your marketing pitch or talk about what you want in the initial communication. If you connect on socials, you might discover that you have a few friends in common. This is a great icebreaker. Mention those friends.

If you are following up via email, say something simple like:

"Dear Leslie, It was nice to meet you. I loved our conversation about music."

Next, OFFER something – a link to an article, an intro to another person who can be helpful, a follow up on whatever you spoke about.

Then close the email with your name and a sig file with links to your site, Instagram Page, Twitter handle, etc.

The first follow-up is always friendly and positive and not business-oriented! Now you have one more possible fan in your online world who is connected to your offline world.

When networking and connecting, don't think about business or music. If you are trying to grow your contacts (and you should always be trying to do this), it's helpful to go to the places that are the exact opposite of your industry. So, as a musician, you would go and network with a bunch of other musicians if you were looking for more people to play with or to tap into a community of musicians. However, this is probably not going to make you money or more fans.

If you go to, say, a bridal convention, and you meet a whole bunch of people who are planning weddings, and you introduce yourself as a musician who plays weddings, you might end up getting some really good gigs. That being said, there are many many reasons to connect with your artist community, and when done right these relationships will be deeply beneficial.

Eli Lev is mentioned several times throughout this book and for good reason. Eli takes considerable time fostering each and every connection he has made, creating truly personal bonds with his tribe. His fans think nothing of it when he texts them a request to pre-save his music or join him on Patreon as a paid monthly subscriber where he currently has almost 100 supporters. A testament to his community connection was the $13,000 he raised from his first Kickstarter campaign that funded his album, Deep South.

Over 1,200 fans follow him on Bandsintown where one said of his livestream, "There's nothing like a show by Eli Lev to uplift you, put you in a good mood, distract you, and remind you to be thankful for all the positive things we have going on in our lives during these uncertain times."

This is a testament to the type of show that Eli puts on and how it affects his fans.

ARTIST HIGHLIGHT:

ELI LEV
Taking Fans Along On An Emotionally Resonant & Uplifting Journey

Instagram: @elilevmusic

Rising singer-songwriter and global citizen Eli is making the world a smaller place, one song at a time. He pens lyrics and melodies for everyday enlightenment — songs that resonate because they're heartfelt, earthy, and offer the wisdom he's gained through lifelong travel and self-discovery. Eli's releases have earned critical praise from many notable publications, and he has received national folk radio support and placement on prominent Spotify playlists. Eli has won multiple industry awards for his work: his second album Way Out West won a Washington Area Music Award (WAMMIE) for best Country / Americana album, while his single "Chasing Daylight" won a grand prize in the SAW Mid-Atlantic Songwriting Competition.

Eli deeply Incorporated his life experiences and created a four-part directional EP series inspired by indigenous traditions he learned while teaching on the Navajo Reservation in Northern Arizona. This, in Eli's words, "has been an incredible guidepost and compass to sustaining my ever growing and evolving music career." Having a personal theme and story to your music and your releases is super important to gaining a strong following and maintaining interest in your music.

Eli takes it one step further - he included his fans in a fan-generated music video that shone a light on his fans by featuring them singing along to his song.

"The belief is that we are surrounded by four directions, and each has unique attributes, power, and teachings. According to the Navajo cosmology, since the sun rises in the east, that is the first direction. With that in mind, I started with All Roads East in the sounds of my youth and upbringing (alt-country / Americana), then I released Way Out West where I experimented with the frontiers of that music (experimental indie folk), and now i've gone back to my southern roots in Deep South with more powerful folk rock and pop sounds."

Eli is on track to make more money in 2021 during a global pandemic than he did in 2019 just from his music alone.

This is an inspiring example of an artist who used IRL PR digitally - what the hell am I talking about? How can it be IRL if it's digital? Note that he showed up to livestreams, went on IG Live and created content around production breakdowns. This is adding a very IRL touch, because it's two people intimately discussing topics on livestreams and IG Lives, so it is IRL because it is intimate. So, if you want to deeply connect with other artists or industry folks there are some powerful tools and lessons suggested here.

So many artists focus on "getting PR," overlooking some possible strategies where some concerted effort will also be inordinately beneficial to your long-term career. Melissa Garcia of Collective Entertainment, Inc. shared this strong advice and inspiration from Sam Dobkin, better known as Trivecta, dance music producer and songwriter from Tampa, FL. He's stylistically known for creating melodic trance, dubstep, bass, and drumstep music.

ARTIST HIGHLIGHT:

TRIVECTA
How He Networked Himself Deeply Into His Artist Community

Instagram: @trivectamusic

Just as it's important to create an engaged community around your fanbase, it's also important as an indie artist to be a part of the artist community, particularly with your peers. This can be in the form of sharing resources / information, promoting one another's new release or show / livestream, or simply engaging with them online or at shows (when that happens again).

By building a strong community, you're not only benefiting from the experiences of other artists, but you're lifting one another. And who knows if a connection will lead to a new creative endeavor. Perhaps you've just met your future producer or collaborator. Or you've gotten along really well with a band that you want to tour with (thereby getting to perform to a wider audience). The allies and network you build within the industry can make a major difference in the growth of your career.

Our client, Trivecta, has done a great job immersing himself within his artist community. He's part of a group of similar artists that collaborate, discuss, and support each other. Here's what he's done with other artists:

- Showed up to livestreams to engage not just with the artist, but with their fanbase.
- Went on IG live with another artist who just released new music.
- Tweeted shout outs about new releases, making sure to tag the artist and share his genuine thoughts about their music.
- Invited artists he collaborates with to participate in promo ideas (i.e. livestreams, production break downs, etc.)
- Wore other artist merchandise when he's performing either live or on a stream.

These are but a few ways you can help elevate other artists.

EXERCISE:

GET WHAT YOU WANT FROM EVERY IRL SITUATION

If you are getting ready to go to a party, a wedding, an event for a friend, whatever.

This exercise takes 5 minutes:

Go to a quiet place.

Take a deep breath.

Focus on what it is you would like today, this week, this month, to move your musical career forward.

If you need to, write down the one or two things you would like.

The default thing you can always ask for is a business card so you can grow your email list.

Keep that thing in mind when you walk out the door.

Really want it? Before you walk in the room, touch your head and repeat to yourself the exact thing / things that you want.

Now follow all of the tips above.

IRL NETWORKING WHILE TOURING

The most important thing you can do on tour is build a base of fans in each market. Before you go on the road, go through all your followers and email newsletter subscribers and organize them by market.

Reach out and connect and offer them something; if the crowds are small enough, maybe they want to join you for a drink before the show and bring a friend. You can check with the club to see if they'll allow people to watch you soundcheck, or hang out after the show.

Cynthia Brando is a Los Angeles singer songwriter who has been described as "equal parts silk and Stevie Nicks." Cynthia has developed a connection with fellow musicians and appreciators as a performer all across the Los Angeles region and beyond, sharing her unique "vintage vibe" powerful vocals and steady acoustic folk rock rhythms in clubs, homes and as a street performer. Cynthia is the founder of Music Emerging, a site dedicated to the emotional well being of people in the music industry.

As you can see, the good will she fosters and her deep relationships create reciprocity on the road and at home.

ARTIST HIGHLIGHT:

CYNTHIA BRANDO
*Blogged Her Way Across The Country Bringing Her
Tribe On Tour*

Instagram: @cynthiabrando

In 2018, I completed my first tour as an independent artist covering 10 states over the summer. I had already been thinking "outside of the box" with publicity since I moved to Los Angeles in 2013 as a complete "newbie." I learned fast, as an independent artist on a limited budget, to take charge of my own career and make my own opportunities.

For several years before my tour, I built up my fanbase by hosting fellow musicians at a house concert series I developed, where I would also open up the show. I started blogging and sharing about my personal experiences in the music industry, street performing, hosting workshops, writing for other music blogs and producing and creating my own music videos. Having interesting and interactive content is key to publicizing not just your music, but your personal story. I did this on my tour by first setting up a travel journal. If you have a website, you can designate a page for a blog and title it to specifically relate to your tour which you can change after your tour is over if you continue blogging. Hosting your blog on a blog hosting site which also has their own community such as Tumblr or Blogger can gain you new fans.

My tour diary became popular as people felt like they were taking the journey with me through my pictures and impressions. You can also include a call to action with a donation link through your PayPal / Venmo, and I offered interesting and personalized postcards from the road that I would send from a unique place. Video blogging is another option. I recorded live shows on a recording device and used Garageband to put them together for a possible live album (Zoom has a wide variety of portable audio recording options). I also livestreamed and had real-time conversations with my fans through several livestreaming platforms. When I was near a national park or an interesting natural wonder, I made iPhone music videos on the road and put them together right from the iPhone iMovie app to share songs from the album I was on tour promoting.

All of the above can be shared through your various social media channels. When I returned from tour, I had a "welcome home" concert where I sold unique items I had bought from my tour; bags from New Mexico, barbecue sauces from Kansas City; moonshine from Mississippi. I sold out and it was a really fun way to end the tour and share my experiences with my fans.

The publicity and outreach I did on that first tour definitely brought me closer to my fans. On my second tour I shared a bill with a duo at a club, Ted and Alice Miller, and they offered me a place to stay, food, and a gig in their town in Nebraska. The gig was successful, and several audience members contacted me afterwards through my website and donated money. I became friends with Ted and Alice and had them on my podcast. I had another fan offer me a house concert in New Mexico. He put me up, fed me, and created one of the most memorable house concerts I have ever performed. He still supports me through Patreon.

This year was supposed to be my third tour, and was going to be an expansion of my previous two tours, but got canceled because of COVID-19. I have used this time to create livestreaming concerts and learn more about publicity. I am releasing singles now and doing publicity and playlisting. I also started my own playlists and include other artists to build community.

ATTEND MUSIC CONFERENCES & INDUSTRY EVENTS

Music conferences and industry events are invaluable when looking to learn and grow in the industry, and there really is an event for everyone. No matter which ones you decide to attend you will have the opportunity to immerse yourself with networking, meet established professionals, and make connections with other artists, all which can be vital to your growth. And there are always music writers and bloggers at conferences. Before you go, look at the attendee list and reach out to schedule a meeting, a coffee, or a cocktail. Be sure to research who each writer is and let them know why you want to meet.

There is also some magic in just seeing who you meet when you get there, if you're the type that likes to roll with it, but if you get anxious in social situations then a little planning ahead is a smart idea.

"Without hesitation, I tell independent artists without representation by a publicist the same thing: get out and meet people face to face. The same way you'd quickly swipe left or right on someone on a dating app without getting to know them is the same way someone can simply delete an email you send them regarding your music. However, it's pretty hard to ignore someone right in front of you. Don't know where to go to meet people? Members of the media are everywhere! Immerse yourself in the things you already love. Go to a lot of shows and panel discussions about media or music issues, and spend your leisure time hanging out at bars or businesses which are music-focused since any music journalist is certainly a music fan as well. The things you enjoy doing, they enjoy just as much! Think like a fan. The media covers things fans want to know about, so be where the fans are. Of course, positioning yourself in the spaces to meet people is half the battle. You also should be prepared to be a social butterfly. Strike up conversations with strangers, introduce yourself to people, and engage in some neutral conversation. Don't only talk about your own music and come off as real-life spam. Carry a well-designed business card. If you keep yourself in venues relevant to your music consistently enough, you'll begin to recognize familiar faces popping up recurrently - it's likely those are the people you want to be talking to." **- Amanda Bassa, Publicist, & Freelance Writer for HipHopDX, XXL, The Source**

PART 6
Hiring A Music Publicist

n case you skipped to this part of the guide and over the part about getting your act together before you try to hire a publicist, here's some gold from one of the most respected members of the music industry, Bruce Houghton, the founder of Hypebot.

"Too often I see developing artists hire a PR person too early and expect them to pluck them from obscurity. PR is telling a story. An artist must develop their story authentically on their own and use it to create a little buzz. A good PR person refines a story, not creates it. A good PR person amplifies buzz, not manufactures it." **- Bruce Houghton, Founder, Hypebot**

29
What A Publicist Does

A music publicist's job is to liaise with the press. In other words, a publicist establishes working relationships between you and those in the media. As already outlined in this guide, media means blogs, playlists, and mostly online publications that are appropriate for you.

A great publicist can make your life easier and accelerate your music career. However, you should not expect your publicist to get you a booking agent, live gigs, a label, or a publishing deal. A savvy and well-connected music publicist may be able to hook you up with other industry connections, but it is not in her job description.

Hiring a publicist should be like hiring another member of your band or adding a critical new member of your team, because that is exactly what you are doing. Everyone on your team has to be on the same page for you to advance.

You have to choose someone you like and who is in alignment with your vision. You also want to make sure the publicist's contact base is right for your genre of music and shares in your short-term and long-term media goals.

THE BENEFITS OF HIRING A PUBLICIST

A publicist will save you a lot of time and work by leveraging her contacts and relationships. A strong publicist will be able to use her hard-won contacts to get you exposure that would otherwise take a lot of time to get on your own. The publicity that she places will help you establish your brand.

Your publicist will increase your name awareness to key media — music bloggers, podcasters, playlisters, music journalists, tastemakers — some of whom are more likely to pay attention to your music if a publicist they know and trust is introducing you.

Additionally, a publicist will get you legitimate press quotes to add to your arsenal to attract more industry attention from booking agents, managers, etc. You should also add these quotes to your website, socials and press kit. If they are strong they will be with you for years to come.

30
What To Expect From A Publicist

WITH PUBLICITY, YOU PAY FOR EFFORT – NEVER FOR RESULTS

Ever heard something like this: "I hired a publicist and I only got three placements. That cost me $1,000 per placement." Unfortunately, this is not how you quantify a publicity campaign.

You pay for the amount of time, effort, and strategy the publicist makes on your behalf. It is up to you to help make sure time, effort, and strategy is part of the equation. Of course, you should get many results. Getting nothing is totally unacceptable. But you never know when your publicist's efforts will show up well after your campaign is complete. Also, if you are smart, you will carefully and thoughtfully build upon any and all relationships that your publicist brings to you, and if you play your cards right you will be able to get your own PR from the same writers and outlets in the future.

"You should know that hiring a publicist doesn't mean you don't have to do any work. Sure, it helps that you have more time to write, rehearse and record; but you should also be active on social media to supplement your publicist's work (and to stay connected with your fans). You should also be prepared to do any phone, video or e-mail interviews your publicist sets up for you." **- Mike Farley, Michael J. Media Group & Concord Records Tour Press**

A publicist is not a miracle worker, but she can introduce you to the media and help you create a defined strategy. Hiring a publicist is just the beginning of your work. You need to keep her busy with stories and angles and events to pitch throughout her time managing your campaign. A music publicist is only as good as whatever she is publicizing, and it is critical to give her as much to use as possible.

"Before hiring a publicist, it might be in an artist's best interests to have all of their materials and current work finished. Nothing helps streamline the start of a PR campaign more than when an artist comes collected and has assets finalized. For example, having your music, bio, press photos, album / single art, and music videos all ready at the beginning of a campaign makes for a smooth start. If you are a new artist, be open to lots of different feature opportunities even from smaller outlets; all initial press when starting out is good press." **- John Cohill, Publicist, Force Field PR**

Just because the agency you hired works for household name artists does not mean you will get in Billboard, Pitchfork, Brooklyn Vegan, Stereogum, NPR Tiny Desk & Rolling Stone.

Publicists should absolutely be hired for who they know and other clients they represent, and their relationships are critical. However, larger bands, on labels with big followings and history (not to mention sales and tours), get placed over smaller, up-and-coming artists. If you are an emerging artist, you need to build up to the larger publications. I have worked with many artists who spent a lot of money for huge PR firms and they were very disappointed with their results.

As already discussed, getting placements has a lot to do with being newsworthy. Simply having a new EP, album, or shows is not grounds for national coverage. Many larger publications may pass you up on your first campaign. This should be considered a building block and not a rejection. So the more appropriate journalists, blogs, and outlets your publicist reaches out to, the better.

If a music publicity firm contacts you, be wary: there are a few shady firms who will contact you from New York or the UK and tell you they "discovered" you on SoundCloud or ReverbNation or Twitter or Spotify or Instagram. The truth is, they troll these sites looking for new music that is posted, then they reach out to see how many artists they can add to their rosters. One of my PR directors worked for a firm that did this and each publicist HAD to reach out to 50 new artists per day or they were fired.

If you hear from a PR firm your ego will love it, but I urge you to run screaming for the hills unless that publicist has a darn good reason for taking the time out of his or her insanely busy schedule to reach out and find you. If they saw you live or they have a legit reason (like they represent a band you are friends with) then, okay – otherwise... It's a PR firm who has been contributing to the commoditization of a highly nuanced process and system that is valuable and precious. These kinds of music publicity firms are hurting firms who do great work with passion and integrity.

31
What To Look For When Hiring A Publicist

Remember, as the artist, you are the buyer, and if you are shopping for music publicity , you're in the driver's seat. It's your art and your money that enables publicists to stay in business. So, do your homework and research well. My team and I speak to a lot of musicians who want publicity. What continues to baffle us is the fact that many of the artists who contact us have no idea what they are actually looking for – someone told them they should "get a publicist" so that's what they do.

FIRST, FIGURE OUT YOUR PR BUDGET

Here's one of my favorite jokes about the music business:

Q: How do you make a small fortune in the music business?

A: Start with a large fortune.

You are calling this PR firm to hire them, so asking about the general ballpark budget is not a bad idea before you get too attached or too deep into a conversation. PR prices vary wildly from a few hundred dollars a month to $5K plus. Most PR firms do not publish their rates. A word of warning: many PR firms try to charge what the client can afford. I have known many wealthy clients or artists with investors or Google-able information about how much money they have, and they pay much more than independent artists with smaller budgets. This is a practice that is alive and well so be mindful and careful not to volunteer too much. I have had many artists tell me right off the bat that they have investors or are willing to pay top dollar. This is not a great idea.

Ask yourself instead: How much money are you willing to spend on publicity? That's the primary question. There are hundreds of music PR firms and individuals who make their livings helping musicians get press. Individuals can charge less than larger agencies who have NYC or Los Angeles overhead and expenses to pay.

"Have a budget, for sure. PR can cost anywhere from $500 / month to a few thousand dollars a month, so please, whatever you do, have a budget for PR when you're getting ready to release." **- Angela Mastrogiacomo, Owner, Muddy Paw PR**

I know that this is extremely broad and therefore not incredibly helpful, but if you have a small budget, being clear and upfront about that will save you time and also keep you from wasting time when asking for proposals from agencies. This process in agency speak is called RFP - Request For Proposal.

"When looking for a publicist, we always recommend doing research first. Ask your friends and fellow musicians, see who represents the artists that inspire you or folks with a similar sound / direction. We only take on projects that we are passionate about and really feel like we can do a great job on, so it has to be a fit." **- Sarah Bennett, Senior Publicist, IVPR**

A solid few minutes on any PR firm's website will reveal a lot. Ask yourself, does this firm represent the kind of music I make? You will want to understand who you are talking to and you won't waste a busy publicist's time. Every PR firm has their roster of clients listed on their website, so make sure you are a great fit and be prepared to tell this to a publicist to show her you understand who you've called.

"I think it's important to research and try to understand what a music publicist does. I might be biased about this but I got started in this business by doing PR for my own band. I would recommend doing this when starting out because it's important to learn how different aspects of the music business (management / PR / booking / radio, etc.) function. It's also a good way to learn what media outlets need from an artist, and it helps to forge relationships with them so you can invite them to your shows or send them new music. *A publicist can create buzz for your band, but it is much more effective to have some buzz already, as a publicist can really help you to capitalize on that." **- Mike Farley, Michael J. Media Group & Concord Records Tour Press**

Set your expectations before you reach out. Most major PR firms (the ones that have national acts on their rosters) have strict criteria for accepting clients and many of them plan campaigns months in advance.

It will be helpful to have reasonable goals in mind that you can talk about. This means figuring out what is attainable from where you are today. Create a list of at least three goals – these should be specific media targets. This way you will know what you are aiming for when you talk to a potential publicist to hire.

32
How To Contact A PR Firm

I get a lot of complaints from artists who call me and say that they have tried to contact certain PR firms and that they never get a response. Speaking in defense of a busy PR firm, many are just too crazed with work to handle all of the incoming inquiries and many don't handle independent artists, preferring to work with represented clients only. With a little finessing, you can get to them. This is not a guarantee that they will take you on as a client, but it will at least get you in the door.

You are the buyer – and therefore in the position of power. You are supplying the music, and you are paying the bill, so you hold the cards. Take your time, do your research, and make sure you're hiring someone who you like and who will do your music and your brand justice.

KNOW SPECIFICALLY WHO YOU ARE CONTACTING

Why are you targeting that firm? You should know the answer to this first and foremost. Visit the "about us" section of the firm's website and read about the team working at the firm so you know who you should be asking for.

If the agency has a contact page there may be specific instructions about how they prefer to hear from new potential clients. Follow them to the letter for best results.

If you find an email address, prepare a short and thoughtful email with who you are, name of project, when you want to release and links to music. A private SoundCloud link is always preferred. One of my clients taught me a fabulous strategy he used. He created an individual playlist per PR firm and he was shocked to discover quite a few wanted to schedule a meeting to discuss working together and they had not listened to any of his tracks.

If you are a telephone kind of person, by all means call. When you make initial contact, don't just dive in and start firing questions at whoever answers. Note that a very busy intern or an administrative assistant may answer the phone and most likely will not be able to tell you prices or availability. And now that practically everyone works from home you may very well be leaving messages. If this is the case, leave a full and concise message including: your name - first and last, and your band / artist name. Your telephone number and your reason for calling – "I am interested in hiring a PR firm and I am inquiring about your interest and availability for a release on (give the date of anticipated release)."

If no one responds within 5 business days, repeat three times. Use the three strikes and they're out method and move on. If a PR firm can't call you back after 3 tries and 15 days they're not the firm for you.

If you do get someone on the phone on first contact, ask only three questions.

But, first introduce yourself very briefly:

Hi, this is _____ and I'm in an indie pop band from _____about to release an EP.

1: Are you considering new clients for the time frame of _____ (your release date?)

2: Give a very brief synopsis of your project, three sentences max. Include:

- The genre of music you play (if you didn't already mention it)
- Distribution plan
- Your release show / tour schedule with markets and highlights
- Then any other parts of your release plan, like your radio promotion, your social media promotions, etc.

3: Ask, "Can I send you the music to consider?" Then send a private SoundCloud link. Do not clog up her inbox with a YouSendIt or a Dropbox link. One click is all she should have to do, unless she requests your music in another format.

If the PR firm is interested, you will set up a call to chat. This is the time when you can really see if you like the publicist, her ideas, and her ability to listen, and this is the time to have a candid conversation about your expectations for the campaign. If she has not listened to the music you sent and checked out your site and socials, or she "yeses" you to death and doesn't talk about expectations, move on.

HAVE THESE 3 TALKING POINTS READY

1. National distribution CD Baby or Tunecore may not be enough of a distribution plan for some larger PR firms.

2. A release date in mind that is at least 2-3 months away from your initial contact.

3. Interesting angles, a charity affiliation, strong newsworthy or niche angles can be enticing for a publicist.

Don't be afraid to ask challenging questions and really have a candid conversation. Ask hard questions to see how she reacts. BE AWARE: A PR firm is NOT a used car lot! I have heard stories that PR firms do "hard sells" saying that rates are only available for a certain amount of time – this means you should be running away.

After the call you should get some sort of a proposal that outlines what you spoke about, the campaign, and the pricing. Take your time to consider this and send back any questions or further points in need of clarification.

Also, ask about the agency's standard contract or agreement. A professional PR firm will have one that you should both sign. The agency should also have terms and conditions and it is your right to see these if you so desire, so you understand if there is a refund policy, and what the expectation is on both sides.

If you do decide to go ahead with the PR firm, asking about accountability and reporting is crucial. You deserve to be updated as your campaign progresses. You want to know who is pitching on your behalf, is it an intern or an experienced publicist? And you should expect regular press reports and updates from your PR team so be sure to ask about the reporting policy. Lastly, ask if they share their pitch lists so you can follow targets on social media and help to strengthen their efforts.

33
Are They Good? How To Do Your Research

9% of publicists all sound fabulous on the telephone, and they should — afterall , communication and sales is their job.

But, sadly, there are a few publicists that are known for not delivering great results, or for being accountable. Therefore, it is critical that you do some due diligence and research.

1. **Google names of each publicist, and the company**, and look for information about these individuals. Dig past the first few pages of results.

2. **Google the different bands and artists that they rep** and search for placements (articles, blog posts). If you don't see articles this may not be a great sign.

3. **Search Glassdoor.** An artist client of mine who was ripped off by a PR firm taught me this technique - search for the name of the company at glassdoor.com and see if anyone who has worked there has reported about what goes on behind the scenes and what the morale is like.

4. **Ask Artists.** Reach out and ask bands on socials.The best part about social media is you can reach out directly to bands and artists on Facebook, Instagram or Twitter and ask what their experience was like. This is the most effective way, as artists will always watch out for other artists.

PART 7
What To Do With Your PR

Music media know one another. If you've made a good impression with one, it might be that much easier to secure a feature with another. Bloggers and playlisters form a giant web. Put your best foot forward, and show appreciation to everyone who features you.

"With so much music and media demanding people's attention, so many artists I have dealt with seem to believe a limited pitch to a blogger will suffice and then no follow up, no sharing of the content, no reply to interview requests, something I understand from bigger artists but for new artists starting on their path, a strong relationship can help both blogger and musician to reach more people." **- Paul Sims, Playlist Curator, Programmer, Music to Shake a Hoof on Musicto**

34
Visualizing Your Publicity Results

It's vital for you to share and publicize every feature you receive, no matter how small. This gets your fans excited, gives you social media fodder, and also makes it clear to music bloggers and journalists that you are going to do something for them. Making a good impression on the writers and outlets who featured you increases your chances of getting more publicity when other bloggers and media check your socials. They are trying to drive traffic to their blogs and you want to demonstrate that you will do your part to help.

"Once you do secure coverage, be sure to share, share, share! You have no idea how much bloggers / writers appreciate a simple share of their posts on social media. By doing so, it not only shows that you value the time they've put into writing about you, but it also benefits both sides. Sharing that feature on your socials opens up the outlet to your fanbase, and vice versa. It's a two-way street, and I think a lot of artists forget that. It also helps develop your rapport with the outlet (because fostering those relationships is important!) and oftentimes leads them to feature you again in the future" **- Erica D'Aurora, Publicist, Muddy Paw PR & Music Blogger, Musical Notes Global, The Honeypop**

LEARN CANVA

There are many tools you can use to simplify your approach to graphic design. At my agency we love Canva because it comes with endless free templates which you can tweak and modify to make all your own. You should visualize every type of feature and playlist add you receive and mix up the way you present placements. Be sure you are staying on brand and within your color schemes and fonts. Highlight choice quotes, display the logo of the outlet with a thank you, include the cover art of the playlist, and grab a screenshot if you so desire.

Canva can magically resize all of your creations to fit each social channel perfectly so that you can post eye-catching visuals on each of your socials. Try using GIFs with movement which will attract more eyeballs.

And don't just share once! You should share placements quite a few times on Twitter as the life of a tweet is very short. You can also share in your stories on Instagram and make a highlight to index all of the press you get so it can be findable for all to see. If you have a really great quote or a choice placement, feature it in a few months as a #TBT or a #FlashbackFriday.

35
Making Your Publicity SEO Friendly

You have shared your placements on your website and on your social media channels and you have tagged all of the writers, publications, and playlisters as well as thanked them all for including you. But there are a few more things you can do with your publicity to make all of the time and effort and money you have invested come back to you by way of Google.

SEO is a whole book in itself, but I want to make sure that you don't just post the graphics you make on your website and think your work is done. The reason for this is you want your press to be indexed by Google and Google can't read text on graphics! If you do include graphics, be sure to add image alt text where possible. To be sure that you get all of the SEO credit you can for quotes, you must include the quotes (or even the whole review) typed out on the press page of your website.

You can additionally link to each article and try to get the media outlets to link to your website. This, sadly, is not foolproof as sometimes music blogs cease publishing and then they go away. You don't want your hard earned reviews and placements to also disappear if that happens.

Add quotes to your EPK. Again, if you are using an outside company to handle your EPK you won't get the SEO. I mentioned this in chapter 13 of this guide but it bears repeating.

For social media, link to your website from all of your social media accounts. Create videos for each of your songs and upload them to YouTube and be sure to optimize your YouTube videos on-platform for SEO.

Add media logos to your site, again adding alt text. Stylistically this may not be for everyone, but many entrepreneurs and companies feature the logos of the news outlets where they were featured on the homepage or media pages of their websites in a way that showcases impressive amounts of press in one glance. If you would like to take a deeper dive into improving your SEO, download Bandzoogle's excellent guide which can easily be found on their site.

36
Showcasing Placements To Your Email List

There are many ways to show off your publicity to your email list. It makes a great talking point, plus, it adds credibility and content!

If you are not already in the habit of sending regular emails and building your list you should deeply consider taking the time and effort to do so as your list is also important when trying to drive pre-saves, Patreon subscribers, and all other types of support.

If you are included on a blog, in a great playlist, or on a podcast and you include the link you are driving traffic to, those outlets and the writers, curators, and hosts will deeply appreciate that you shared their hard work with others and introduced them to new fans.

If you get multiple placements, space them out and add one highlight to every single email you send.

"One of our clients made a habit of sharing her choice press quotes with her email list and she got booked by two promoters including a festival in her hometown as a result of showcasing her local publicity." **- Jamie Alberici, VP, Cyber PR**

37
Gaining Leverage With Club Owners And Agents

Al Laughlin is a client and friend who is near and dear to my heart. Al was the keyboard player in The Samples and my first real job in the music business was working at his record label What Are Records? Fast forward 20+ years and Al now has a new band called Highway 50 and I was honored to be back as his publicist.

When Al hired me, we had a frank conversation about what his publicity goals were. He was already very well known from his contribution to one of the most beloved bands from his home state of Colorado, but he was having trouble getting his new project booked as many fans didn't know he was in a new band. We worked with local and regional Colorado press to expand awareness, and every time we placed an article or a review, Al strategically shared it with a small list of venue owners and promoters that he had carefully curated.

He included a personal note and then showed off the article to prove to the bookers that he had a PR firm who was working hard for him and that if he was booked for a gig he would continue to publicize to bring fans to the shows. Our strategy worked and he got more bookings.

You would be amazed at how few artists actually identify strategies like this, yet when applied and executed they work.

38

Gaining Leverage With Music Industry VIPs

Club owners and promoters may not be an end goal for you as they were for Al and Highway 50. You may be trying to get the attention of a manager, booking agent, distributor, label or publicist like my friend John. Here's our story:

One of my favorite humans and one of the most successful indie musicians I know is John Taglieri. I met John 21 years ago when he cold-called my office. The conversation went something like this:

John: Hi Ariel, my name is John Taglieri and I'm an indie musician from New Jersey. I have been following your firm and your work and I really love what you are doing! I'm not yet in a position to hire you, but I will be someday. I'd love to take you for coffee.

Me: Hi John, it's nice to meet you (inner voice - I don't go for coffee with artists I've never met). I'm afraid I don't have time for coffee but let's stay in touch.

John: That sounds great! I will be in touch!

Me: OK. Bye.

A few weeks later guess who called? YEP! John. This time he had an offer that was so generous and thoughtful I couldn't refuse.

Round 2

John: Hi! I've been playing all over the state of New Jersey and I have built up a killer media list of all of the best music writers, TV, and radio DJs in the state who support indie rock musicians like me - would you like me to send it to you?

Me: Thanks John, that's so generous - it's hard to find media who cover indie artists in many areas of New Jersey.

He sent the list fully annotated with who to call first, and his contacts were excellent.

The third time John called me he invited me to join him to see his friend Jeffery Gaines, who was playing at the BB King Blues Club where I was the PR Director. We met up and we became fast friends. He did, indeed, hire me to be his publicist the very next year. I, in turn, hired him when he was off the road to work on my team, and now two decades later I'm about to publicize his upcoming release.

John also became indispensable to his college booking agent and he got booked dozens of times on huge gigs because he was dependable and would show up at the last minute when other bands had cancelled. He made himself totally available and did it all with gratitude and grace and it paid off for years.

You can be like John and leverage relationships you don't even have yet. I have a few clients who have very smartly created a VIP list for the music industry. This is different from their regular email list which goes to fans. They carefully curate emails 4-6 times a year to keep people in the music business up to date with their growth as they develop and they include the press that they have received. They also include milestones such as social media follower growth, email list growth, and placements in film and TV.

You don't have to create a whole list to use this leverage strategy, you can simply make a list of a handful of important contacts and be sure to reach out to them a few times a year.

EXERCISE:

HOW TO GET TO ANYONE IN THE MUSIC BUSINESS

Here is the 7-step plan outlined for music industry targets:

1. The name of the VIP

2. What is their position in the industry

3. Social media links - follow them across all channels

4. Topics (or many preferably) that are the impetus for why you are reaching out

5. A few sentences about why they should care or how you can help them

6. What you are sharing - links, stats, quotes, social numbers, tickets sold, etc.

7. How the VIP likes to be contacted and how often you should follow up, etc.

This is a great way to stay on people's radars and to network in a respectful manner. If you can think of any way to help them (see step 5) this leaves an indelible impression and could lead to a life-changing relationship.

PART 8
Publicity In The New World

COVID-19 has had a massive impact across the entire music industry. At the time of this book's publication, it's predicted that things may be getting back to normal sometime during this summer or fall. Whether or not this happens remains to be seen, but one thing that this pandemic has unveiled is - you probably could benefit from a stronger digital presence and strategy.

Many touring and session musicians have had their livelihoods dwindle with cancellations of shows and tours. Some have found ways to pivot and have become online content curators and creators and they are building up new audiences, connecting with old and redefining how they approach releasing and fan building.

Keeping all of this in mind is key when launching your publicity campaign or discussing strategy with a publicist. You want to be sure that you are taking extra time to be mindful and considerate with your pitches, timing, and angle. My team at Cyber PR had to stop and restart a lot of our campaigns to account for the pandemic, the election, the events of January 6th, and the Inauguration. Being flexible is key nowadays.

"Journalists are people first and they are going through the pandemic too. Although they are in the media business, they have families, dreams, and aspirations that may be compromised at the moment. Maybe they are doing just fine - you never know. Keep this in mind when you approach them and pitch stories. Ask how they are doing first before telling them what you want. Check in with them when you don't need anything. Publicity has always been a people and relationship business and during hard times, that aspect is even more crucial. In general, we all want to work with people we like and those that are kind and supportive. Be that publicist or artist they look forward to working with and hearing from." **- Heather Youmans, PR Manager, Fender Guitars, Former *LA Times* Media Group Journalist, Singer-Songwriter**

The pandemic has also shifted the landscape for publicity and there are some interesting possibilities and options for artists who did not "qualify" in the eyes of many publicists pre COVID-19. Many of my publicist friends have told me that they are now weighing their choices on who they represent differently, as a developed online audience and creative approach is now more newsworthy than ever before and a positive attitude won't hurt either.

"Before the pandemic, my standards for taking on artists were that they were touring in markets besides their hometowns. Now, it's become important that they have an encouraging attitude because the world needs that. Musicians are a 21st Century answer to Fiorello LaGuardia, who read the comics to families during the Great Depression. I'm promoting artists who are trying to help make the world a better place. I think now those acts have a built-in advantage over those that are what I'll call entitled — the ones that are expecting the world to give to them. Nowadays, you can't do that. Artists are being asked to make their tribe feel better. We have to create cool media events and collaborate with others. Folk Alliance is using the word "unity" when they set up online events for their members. Publicists should also be promoting social media events now, as those get-togethers will help give their fans and them a great sense of community." - **Anne Leighton, Publicist, Anne Leighton Media & Music Services**

Jazz artist Monika Herzig started livestreaming due to the fact that her promo tour was cancelled, and a new radio show was born. She now has the opportunity to shine a light on other artists who she will no doubt be performing and collaborating with IRL when the world opens back up.

ARTIST HIGHLIGHT:

MONIKA HERZIG
A COVID-19 Silver Lining - Creating Of "Talking Jazz"
Radio Show

Instagram @monikaherzig

In 1987, the pedagogical institute in Weingarten Germany, awarded a scholarship for a one-year exchange program at the University of Alabama to jazz pianist Monika Herzig. Together with her partner and guitarist Peter Kienle, she arrived in the States on a one-way ticket, with one suitcase of belongings and one guitar. Since then, she has completed her Doctorate in Music Education with minors in Jazz Studies at Indiana University, where she is now a faculty member in Arts Administration. As a touring jazz artist, she has performed at many prestigious jazz clubs and festivals, including Jazz Fest, Cleveland's Nighttown, Birdland, and the Manchester Craftsmen's Guild.

She has released more than a dozen CDs under her leadership on her own ACME Records, as well as Owl Studios, and Whaling City Sounds. Her awards include a DownBeat Magazine Award for Best Original Song, a Jazz Journalist Association Hero award, as well as grants from the NEA, the Indiana Arts Commission, MEIEA, among others. She is also an author of two books; David Baker: A Legacy in Music, and Experiencing Chick Corea: A Listener's Companion.

From Monika:

"I was in the middle of a CD release tour for our newest album "Eternal Dance" (Savant) with my all-female jazz instrumentalist group Monika Herzig's Sheroes, when we hit the wall at the Keystone Corner in Baltimore, on March 15, and had to return to our homes.

Initially, we thought we should pull the plug on the album and find a new release date after this is over. But the radio campaign had just gotten started and a big review in DownBeat Magazine was scheduled for the June issue, so we let it go its course. It turned out that the album received huge support in the radio world and stayed in the JazzWeek Top 50 for 15 weeks peaking at #6.

The sudden split of the group and loss of live performances turned into a huge learning curve on technology as I started livestreaming regularly with my guitarist husband and exploring tools to create collaborative recordings and other content. Initially, our backdrop and lighting and sound were terrible and we had to buy a bunch of equipment to improve the settings.

Out of the blue, the radio station manager from WETF in South Bend, Indiana, called me to ask if I wanted to produce a show for them. Initially, the idea was not appealing at all to me — more technology, more work, more things to learn. But the more I thought about it, I remembered all the cool things I had discovered from various radio shows and podcasts. So, I took the plunge into recording interviews with artists I work with and admire, about their music and specific aspects to listen to before playing a track. The show is called "Talking Jazz" and airs twice a week on WETF in South Bend, Indiana, and online at wetfthejazzstation.org.

In addition, I started a YouTube playlist, Talking Jazz, where I produce the interviews as videos with pictures and extra sound clips for archiving. It'll take a bit of time to spread the word and build the followers, but it sure is a great way to showcase some of the best music that's out there, in my opinion. Eventually, I'm hoping to add live performance with some of these artists to the shows once we can get back together.

"Now is a time when community-building is more important than ever. Whether or not your tribe is large or small, your fans look to you and your music for guidance, comfort, and sometimes just for distraction. You are an influencer. Use your influence to help others in these difficult times." **- Bruce Houghton, Editor, Hypebot**

There are publicity opportunities when you use livestreaming to be creative and you think about what can be newsworthy. Pick up any publication nowadays and the calendar listings and live event sections have been replaced by suggestions on what to stream.

"I have seen some interesting shifts away from tour press. First, with livestreaming, you aren't confined to the market your gig is in. I recently landed coverage in Maine, Texas, and California for an artist based in Chicago. Second, writers who write about live shows are doing more music reviews and interviews — especially because those artists are still making music and wanting to get it out there. Third, some outlets have come up with new and unique features for musicians and bands — i.e. asking them to curate Spotify playlists that have a theme (like songs about rain, or songs that influenced your band); or to write up your best and worst gig experiences; or to write up your favorite shows to binge while quarantining. One client of mine did a virtual happy hour once a week where they hung out with fans on Facebook, had drinks, and maybe played a song or two." **- Mike Farley, Michael J. Media Group & Concord Records Tour Press**

Like many artists who relied on touring for their main income, Joe Deninzon had to pivot to adapt to COVID-19. He revamped his website, putting focus on the fact that you can hire him to record entire string sections for your next album. While on the road, he has an amazing curated show concept.

Joe's publicist, Anne Leighton, has said: "I look at every concert or show as a special event. With collaborative dates, we've given them a name-- the SonicVoyageFest, so we have more to work with in publicizing these shows. Plus I'm collaborating with other people in spreading the word. I like getting photos, logos, one paragraph bios from each group, plus a few YouTube videos. I think prog people tend to connect the most on social media which works to our advantage."

ARTIST HIGHLIGHT:

JOE DENINZON
The Creation Of The SonicVoyageFest - Curated Shows

Instagram: @joedeninzon

Joe has been hailed by critics as "The Jimi Hendrix of the Violin," because of his innovative style on electric seven-string violin. His band Stratospheerius has released five albums. He can be heard on over a hundred CDs and jingles as a violinist and string arranger. A BMI Jazz Composer's grant recipient and winner of the John Lennon Songwriting Contest, he has written "Concerto for Seven String Electric Violin and Orchestra" with the Muncie Symphony Orchestra. He also wrote Plugging In, a book on electric violin techniques for Mel Bay Publications. Joe holds Bachelor's degrees in Violin Performance and Jazz Violin from Indiana University and a Master's in Jazz / Commercial violin from Manhattan School of Music.

I am the lead singer / electric violinist in the progressive rock band Stratospheerius.

In recent years, we've been successfully convincing venues to let us curate our own nights.

Most often, we create a "night of prog," inviting bands in our little scene who we have befriended to share the bill with us. The cross-promotion is great, the attendance has always been bigger than when we were blindly asking a venue to give us a 45-min slot, and each band gains new fans. Plus it's a great way to trade shows with bands in other markets you want to break into. The shows have brought more people when we did them live, and even though we were playing in clubs, we did walk away with more cash in our pockets than we used to before we started curating.

Lately, I've been curating mini "electric string festivals," making people aware of all the creative electric string players out there writing their own original music. This has helped our social channels and newsletter to grow. In the future when the world opens back up we hope to make the Electric String Festival an event that takes place all over the country with different creative electric string artists I know. Places like Nashville, LA, and Austin, TX.

During the pandemic, I have been doing monthly shows online for numerous festivals that are livestreaming, as well as a recent concert series for NY-area health workers called "Music for the Soul." I will also be creating a virtual Electric String Fest.

We live by the idea that "rising tides lift all boats." Don't wait to be a part of a scene, make your own.

39
Making Your Livestreams Shine

N ow that we are over a year in it has become clear that even as the pandemic wanes, livestreaming will not.

"It goes without saying that livestreaming is the new norm and if you have not taken the leap, now is the time. The best part of creating a livestream schedule and adhering to it is you will quickly realize who your superfans are. The people who you only saw a few times a year on tour now have the opportunity to see you more often than ever before. One of my clients who toured Europe every other year now has her European superfans tuning in every time she plays. Another received a $500 tip from a fan who was happy to support him and even happier to see him many times on multiple streams. You don't only have to stream live music — you can host a happy hour, a live Q&A, a music masterclass, or an interview with another artist you admire. The more creative you get, the more publicity opportunities could open up." **- Mike Farley, Michael J. Media Group & Concord Records Tour Press**

If you have not not taken the plunge or recently tuned up your livestream game, here are some things to consider as you do.

CONDUCT A TRIAL RUN

Make sure the audio and visual are decent. You could purchase expensive equipment for the utmost quality, but plugging a microphone into your computer and shooting video with an iPhone may be more than adequate if you are skilled.

SET A VIBE

Make sure you are setting some kind of vibe - hang up a sheet, some seamless paper or posters or drape a lamp with a colored scarf, but make sure you are not streaming from a place that will cause your viewers to focus on the background (they will if it's distracting), pay attention to details like open closet doors or people walking into the frame, or even things that should be hidden like cords, exit signs, etc.

GET GREAT LIGHTING & A BACKDROP

Ring lights are great and they make everyone look better. You can get a full ring light setup online for approximately $100. If you want a backdrop (if you don't have a nice looking corner of your home or studio), buy a stand and you can switch seamless paper rolls or even use cool wrapping paper when you want to change colors and vibes.

DRESS THE PART

I know it's tempting, but I also know that you probably don't show up for all your gigs in sweats and a t-shirt, do you? Be mindful of choosing colors that pop so you can be seen, and remember your streams may very well be posted across your socials and seen well into the future so putting thought into your wardrobe is worth it. If you are performing in front of a dark / black background and you are wearing black or a similar color to the background you will look like a weird floating head.

CREATE CONSISTENCY

Create a livestream schedule and stick to it. Being consistent is crucial to succeeding at the livestream game. Check your analytics to see when your fans are most likely to be on social media and cater to them.

MAKE IT NEWSWORTHY

Give fans and media a reason to want to stream. Create themed setlists including fun covers, invite guest performers to join, interact with viewers holding Q&A sessions. Keeping shows different and fun each time will help bring back fans and create audience growth. Perhaps give proceeds to charity to tie in a cause.

40
Livestream Platforms
To Consider

There are numerous streaming platforms to choose from, and you can earn revenue either by selling tickets or asking for donations. Don't be afraid to be honest with your fanbase. You deserve to get paid, so don't be shy about sharing your Patreon, PayPal, Venmo, CashApp, or any other links during your streams. If you feel you are genuinely not ready for tips, use your streams to build your list.

STAGE.IT

Stage.It (stageit.com)has been hosting digital concerts for years. It is free to use but they do keep a percentage of your sales. The viewer can either purchase a ticket, or "hitch a ride" – this will let other ticket-buyers know that you're searching for a ticket and if you're lucky maybe someone will buy one for you. The video will not be saved after you stream and fans will have an added opportunity to tip you during your stream.

TWITCH

Twitch (twitch.tv): Gamers have been using it for years. If you are willing to do long format and spend a lot of time on this platform with consistency, then you could make a nice income on Twitch. It has built-in revenue options. Bandsintown has partnered with Twitch so you can become an affiliate and get up to speed quickly.

CROWDCAST

You must buy a monthly subscription but Crowdcast (crowdcast.io) offers easy integration to your website where you can build a password-protected page for your fans. Fans will have access to a replay, and you can also download a video of your livestream for guests to watch later if they missed the stream or want to re-watch. It integrates with your Patreon so that you can host live broadcasts limited to just your patrons.They take fees but you can sell tickets without getting charged commission through your Bandzoogle website.

Zoom The entire free world learned how to Zoom when the pandemic hit and it can be a great solution if you like interacting with your fans. Pay for the upgrade so your livestreams can be more than the 40-minute cut-off.

SIDE DOOR

Side Door (sidedooraccess.com) is a brilliant secure Zoom integration where you can see the audience and they can see each other. It's not just a performance, it's an impromptu community. They pay out Performing Rights Orgs like ASCAP / BMI / SOCAN on your behalf. Work alone or split revenue right at the point of sale with online Presenters who can help you sell more tickets.

Only relying on tips or donations is the first step in generating real revenue. You must also alert your viewers that there are more available options by mentioning that you have other offers available.

Plan when you will do this when mapping out the format of your livestream so it doesn't seem like an afterthought when you ask. Many artists are truly uncomfortable with asking for money so rehearsing a way to make it land in a non-sales-sounding way may be a powerful strategy for you.

41
Monetize Before You Publicize

B efore you jump straight to publicizing your livestreams ask yourself - have you set yourself up to monetize first? This is important to put into place before you take the time to drive PR and views. In response to COVID-19, many services have stepped in to help musicians make money by monetizing their livestreams.

"Encourage them to buy your music directly (i.e. from BandCamp or your merch store). And speaking of merch, you can do a special sale or release a limited run of a new design."
- Melissa Garcia, Manager, Collective Entertainment, Inc.

Contribute Some or All to Charities: There are many amazing charities that help musicians specifically such as Sweet Relief, MusiCares, and Help Musicians. There are also many charities that are feeding kids or families in need. You can contribute some of your earnings and this may make asking feel more comfortable for you.

Here's the rundown of tools you are probably already using and how you can optimize them for monetizing livestreams.

INSTAGRAM

IG is the musician's favorite platform and I bet you use IG Live. Instagram doesn't offer a tool for accepting payments for monetizing music livestreams so you'll have to get clever.

Making Your One Instagram Link Count: Update your link in your Instagram bio to include multiple links including one where fans can pay you and another where they can buy merch. Two tools for this are:

Linktr.ee – add all of your payment links, highlight your other socials, invite email sign ups and even add a video.

Lnk.bio – gives you a clean white page where you can type anything you want.

ASK FOR A CONTRIBUTION OLD-SCHOOL STYLE

During his IG Livestreams Eli Lev pans over to where fans can find him online and tip using a whiteboard. It's simple and effective.

FACEBOOK

Rich Genoval Aveo, who is my next artist highlight, has been crushing the game of monetizing livestreams. He consistently streams four times a week at 5:30 PM and his wife, artist Cat London, often joins him. They take piano bar style requests. He has branded the series the Pandemic Piano Party (PPP) and he skinned the livestream video to highlight the tip jar. He crossposts on YouTube so his fans can view there as well, and he has a VIP offer where they will record a custom Happy Birthday or any type of special song and message for $20.

I asked Rich how he set up his tech and here is what he shared:

"My stream is pretty standard. I use this freeware app called "OBS" to produce the stream, and a multicast system called "Castr" to multicast it to YouTube and Facebook. The learning curve might be a little steep at first, but once you learn the ins and outs (I'm still quite the beginner at it, and learned everything on YouTube), it's pretty simple to navigate. Of course, using some decent lighting and sound gear doesn't hurt. For the ads...I created the banner graphic myself, and within OBS I can cue up when the banner comes up, etc....as it's a production suite where you can switch scenes, etc...it's definitely doing a little something!"

YOUTUBE LIVE

As long as your YouTube channel is verified you can go live on YouTube using a desktop or a mobile phone. Unless you are an experienced YouTuber, monetizing is not that easy, as it happens through super chat as part of their partner program, or you can rely on ads, which will pay you pennies, or request tips and donations and merch sales (like you do on IG and Facebook Live). When your stream is over, it will automatically be saved to your YouTube channel.

PERISCOPE

If Twitter is your social media platform of choice then using Periscope is a no-brainer as it integrates seamlessly with Twitter and your stream will show up to all who follow you on Twitter.

BANDZOOGLE – SELL TICKETS

If you are a Bandzoogle member you can sell tickets commission-free through your website in order to start monetizing your livestreams. The added functionality for virtual and streaming ticketing allows you to include a livestream link and password. This will be sent automatically to your fans once they purchase a ticket. Bandzoogle is offering this commission-free, and payments go directly to you.

SOUNDCLOUD – USE DIRECT SUPPORT LINKS

SoundCloud has added direct support links so fans can help you. Direct support links create a "Support Artist" highlight box on your SoundCloud profile which allows fans to pay you or donate to your crowdfunding campaign. SoundCloud is not taking a fee for this service and you can connect to Paypal, Shopify, Patreon, Bandcamp, Cash.app, Kickstarter, or GoFundMe.

BANDCAMP – SELL BUNDLES

One great incentive you can put together for your fans is a bundle of goodies that you can plug during livestreams. Bandcamp allows you to put together all of the music you've ever released, plus offer monthly features like special releases and discounts on merch. You can have your fans pay a one-time fee or pay by the month.

SPOTIFY – CREATE AN ARTIST FUNDRAISING PICK

Artist Fundraising Pick allows you to pin a payment destination where your fans can tip you. Spotify for Artists admin users select Get started on the banner at the top of their dashboard to submit their Fundraising Pick. You'll be directed to a page where you can input your $cashtag, PayPal.me, or GoFundMe link.

VENMO & PAYPAL QR CODES

Venmo's in-app QR codes, which are automatically generated when you make an account, are an easy way to let your fans know where they can tip you. Not everyone uses Venmo though, so it's important to give your fans multiple places that they can contribute to you. We recommend PayPal's in-app QR code that goes directly to your PayPal. Me link. If you haven't made a PayPal.Me link yet, do that to access your QR code. Open the PayPal app and click the "More" icon on the bottom right. Click "Get paid with QR codes" and your QR code will pop up. Save it to your camera roll and start sharing!

PATREON

Patreon offers your fans ownership of the project and makes them feel more connected to you. It also builds a community that you can form deep bonds with and gives you something that will bring you ongoing income to ask for during livestreams. More than 30,000 creators (of all types, not just musicians) launched in the first 3 weeks of March 2020 alone, and these new creators are acquiring patrons faster than usual. You will need to educate your fans on what it is and how to use it.

In April 2020, as the reality of the pandemic really began to hit home, I was surfing Facebook Live one evening and came across something really special. It was my past client Rich and his wife bantering with and taking requests from a captivated audience. It immediately became clear that this livestream was different than the countless others I'd come across. And, the best part was I could tune in the next night and the night after that.

ARTIST HIGHLIGHT:

RICH GENOVAL AVEO
How Creating The Pandemic Piano Party Solidified His Brand & Artistry

Instagram: @richaveo

Rich Genoval Aveo is a singer-songwriter, pianist, and empowerer. Based in the New York / New Jersey area. Rich has led a creative and passionate life on his terms, making people smile along the way. He feels the world operates at its best when people are elevated, and believes music and quality entertainment elevate like nothing else. His mission is to positively impact as many people as humanly possible through his artistic expression and make people feel inspired to live their best lives. In 2012, he quit his lucrative day job to pursue his passion full time, and never looked back. So one morning in 2012 - on what was probably his 400th morning in bumper to bumper traffic on the Garden State Parkway - he decided - "My real story starts today." And he went into the office that morning and gave his two-week notice. Today he's a full time musician making a full-time living.

My whole mantra is "if you're not growing, you're dying" so from the first day of quarantine here in New Jersey / New York, I knew I'd need to adapt if I wanted to continue to elevate people with live music.

My primary gig is live entertainment, and with all venues closed down indefinitely, I knew something was going to have to change, and I would have to spring into action quickly. I refuse to be one of those people who kept wishing and waiting for things to 'go back to the way it was'. That has never been the way to progress.

My primary focus during the quarantine has been live performance with my show, "The Pandemic Piano Party (PPP)." And as far as promotion, I have taken a rather aggressive approach to spreading the word - possibly more than ever - even before the quarantine. Mostly direct marketing to my existing fanbase, and unifying the brand across all platforms. I run three separate websites, and this show is linked to the home page of each one. I keep an updated daily link to my show on all my socials.

This is unusual for me, because for years I had separated my businesses into separate universes, (original artist, live event band, and one-man theater show), The PPP has been a nice through-line tying them all together rather smoothly. I've developed a 'what have I got to lose' mentality, which has actually served quite well!

With the growing success of The Pandemic Piano Party, I am introducing a new segment where I cover a song from my favorite unsigned artist friends. Being as my show is primarily request-based, I want to take a moment to tip my hat to - and introduce my fans to - some of my fellow talented, independent songwriters. In this new segment, I will be talking a bit about the artist, featuring their links to their newest releases, and directing people on how to purchase / support them.

I'm working on some innovative ways to make it exciting and fit the show format like segment graphics, etc...and will turn this into a recurring theme. Having me learn and cover their songs in my show format has been very exciting for everyone. It's still a work-in-progress, but it's a great way to introduce a whole new supportive community to my talented cohorts!

Simply put, In the face of this global pandemic attitude is everything. And because of how scary this has all been, it's actually made me more fearless than ever. Which I think is the ultimate adaptation. Evolution takes courage and a burning desire to survive. And if we can survive this, I'm pretty sure we can survive anything.

Granted, it has been a lot of work, emotionally, spiritually and physically, but to watch this community grow and express how they have a safe place to let go of their worries, it has completely shifted my mindset on how to PR and market my mission. It has unified the brand and made my overall PR mission even more clear.

42
Livestream Publicity

M any music publicists have shared that they managed to get publicity for their clients' livestreams and this will be possible once you build up a strong audience or if you create livestreams that are newsworthy.

"Every response from a journalist is treasured more now than ever. However, it's not all doom and gloom. Now has also been a great time for artist creativity. Time off the road and away from promo schedules is driving more music and livestreaming which all helps with publicity. There are definitely new opportunities in the world of social media and TV for artists to tap into! Now is a time of persistence and patience with PR - finding the balance between the two is an art we as publicists need to continue to perfect." **- Doug Hall, Founder, Big Feat PR**

Here's a rundown of what to do to start the publicity wheels turning for your livestreams:

VISUALIZE YOUR LIVESTREAM ANNOUNCEMENTS

Make sure these match your brand and style. These will be added to all of your socials, your blog or news section, and your website

PREP YOUR WEBSITE

Change the artwork on the landing page to announce the livestream schedule. Add an announcement to the news section if you have one and add mention of the livestream schedule to the Bio / About section with a link to stream (studies show people tend to take action on the Bio page!). Also, add to your blog if you have one.

SEND DEDICATED LIVESTREAM NEWSLETTERS

Something very telling happened when the pandemic started. Artists who had taken the time to build, maintain and use their email lists had a much easier time adjusting to the new realities. So, if you have not taken the time to work on your mailing list now is the time. Survey your subscribers for feedback on what platforms they want to see you on and what times work for your audience. Make ONE CTA per email for your fans such as:

- Add my upcoming livestream to your calendar
- RSVP here link
- Follow me on Bandsintown so you never miss an update
- Join my Patreon community for exclusive livestreams

POST ON YOUR SOCIALS

Instagram: Change your bio to announce your livestreams, Add a link to schedule in your linktr.ee. Create a livestream tile and post. Create multiple livestream Stories and video snippets and post past livestreams to give your fans a preview of what to expect. Also, create tiles to spread out over the next few weeks with different fun ways to announce. Build Hashtag Clouds on the notes section of your phone and add them as the first comment (you can add up to 30 including your hashtags in the comment!) Start the comment with 5 periods and returns. Use the IG Hashtag Expert for IG app to help generate clouds.

Facebook: Upload a new banner to both your Facebook personal profile and Page, announcing your livestreams. Edit the "About" section to include the livestream schedule and make a mini banner with "LIVESTREAM SCHEDULE." Post a status update announcing your livestream(s), and pin it to the top as a timeline feature.

Boost or buy an ad: If you don't already have your credit card set up on Instagram and Facebook to purchase promoted posts and ads, register so you can easily boost posts.

Twitter: Make sure the top banner, profile picture, and bio reflect your livestream schedule. Tweet out your livestream announcements. Pin the tweet to the top of your profile. Create 5 separate tweets announcing in 5 ways.

EXAMPLE TWEETS AND STORIES:

We are going LIVE on (date) at (time) on (platform)! We'll be doing (x) songs. Reply with some requests! (link to platform)

If you're not busy this (day), come join our #virtualconcert on (platform) at (time)! We'd love to see you there. (heart emoji) (link to platform)

We miss performing so much! That's why we've decided to do a live show for you via (platform)! The show is (day) at (time) - please join us! (link to platform)

We're going LIVE on (platform) at (time) on (day)! Retweet this for a chance to join the livestream with us and ask a question (rock on emoji) (link to platform)

We're livestreaming! Come hang with us (day) on (platform) at (time)! Drop some requests below (smile or fun emoji) (link to platform)

YouTube: Customize the top banner, profile picture to announce livestream. Upload and annotate past livestreams.

Bandsintown: Add your livestreams to your schedule. Post to trackers to announce the shows. Ask fans to upload photos of your livestreams on your profile. Ask fans to post a review of your stream which can also be used to build quotes for your EPK.

Snapchat: snap the release and share!

LinkedIn: at the top in your summary section, add your livestream schedule.

TikTok: in order to go live on TikTok you must have 1,000 followers - so get to growing on this platform! It is the fastest growing app right now, and it's a giant hub for indie musicians. If you're over 18, people who are watching your livestream can send you "gifts" - digital currency that can be turned into cash. You can add an announcement when you go live and it will show up at the top of all of your followers' notifications and feed.

Once you have all of your promotions in place for your livestreams and you have created something that is newsworthy around your streams, you should try to get publicity. If there is a newsworthy angle and a full livestream schedule, I suggest a press release, and if you have local charities involved you should absolutely go for a local or regional publicity campaign. Also, try for niche outlets if your themes fit the bill.

PART 9
Conclusion

We have all heard the phrase "all publicity is good publicity." It's beneficial to truly understand this and the truth is the average person remembers very little of what they read. They are not going to remember a lukewarm review. Also, many will never remember how large the outlets that covered you are, only what was said. A strong quote from the media is beneficial no matter what outlet it comes from so don't worry about who will cover you to start. Dive in and learn the process as it's almost exactly the same no matter what level you are at today and as you build the outlets will follow.

43
Your Publicity Is Yours Forever

Publicity is an ongoing process. It will ebb and flow as you release and as newsworthy occasions and opportunities cross your path. There will be times when you will actively endeavor to seek publicity with your time and effort or money, and there will be times when publicity may come in when you least expect it. In all cases, it is an integral part of your big picture as a musician.

I recently had a discussion with a new client who had a beautiful quote on her SoundCloud page. The quote was so powerful and well-written it made me stop and listen to her music immediately. When I told her how much I loved the quote there was dead silence on the other end of the phone.

"But I got that quote over 10 years ago," she said.

So what? It doesn't matter. The quote is timeless and it captures her spirit and her music and it's hers to use forever.

Right before the pandemic closed all live music venues in New York, I went to see a past client, who I had run a publicity campaign for in 2001, perform at Joe's Pub.

On the marquee outside the venue was a huge beautiful poster depicting her on stage with her arms spread open wide and her head thrown back. There, splashed under her image in bold letters, was a fabulous quote that I had placed for her 19 years prior. The quote was perfect and it could have run in the paper that very day. I smiled from ear to ear as I collected my ticket and walked into the venue to enjoy the show.

COME VISIT CYBER PR MUSIC

There are over 300 blog posts that cover many other aspects of music marketing, social media, and promotion for musicians at my website cyberprmusic.com. If you would like to start a conversation with me there, please do.

ABOUT THE AUTHOR

Ariel Hyatt runs Cyber PR Music, an artist development, social media, & content strategy firm based in New York City. Her agency just celebrated 25 years in business and she and her all-female team of women who get sh-t done run digital PR campaigns and advise on how to create online influence and release impactful projects. She has spoken in 12 countries to over 100,000 creative entrepreneurs and is the author of five bestselling books on social media, marketing, and crowdfunding including *Cyber PR for Musicians*, *Music Success in 9 Weeks*, and *Crowdstart*.

She is an obsessive world traveler and live music junkie, hoping that both things will be things again in the near future. She splits her time between NYC and Lee, MA, with her husband, son, and gray tabby Hunter C. Thompson (the C stands for cat) because everyone should live with a snarky music journo.

Acknowledgments

Deepest thanks and all my love to my husband Erskine C. Childers for being my partner, my rock, and my sanity in this crazy, pandemic, co-parenting life.

To my amazing core team of badass women, Jamie Alberici and Kayla Coughlan your great spirits and hard work to keep Cyber PR humming. You are the best co-workers I've ever had.

Melissa Nastasi for all of your innovative, hard-earned publicity and your amazing attitude.

Suz Paulinski for filling so many roles - collaborator, TTU writer, music biz shrink, COO, and confidant.

Lorne Behrman for being the most reliable and consistent bio writer I've ever worked with. Your enthusiasm, empathy, and excellent writing over the years make our team's work easier.

Joyce "Rock On" Dollinger Esq. for always watching out for me and for always being by my side for not only legal help, but also as a true friend.

Jayme Johnson of Worthy Marketing Group for your keen eye, honesty, and all of your help in bringing this book to light.

Kristin Fayne Mulroy for being my best friend since I was 5 and also for copy editing this book with so much love.

Lindsey Barbara for stepping in at all the perfect moments when we need you.

Marni Wandner for being my Brooklyn and Fire Island walking partner, Gemini twin and sounding board in the crazy business.

Susan White-Ahl for your constant love and support.

Derek Sivers for always answering the phone and picking up exactly where we left off whether it's been a week or a year.

To Ilyana and all the women of Ladies Social, my amazing network of indomitable spirits who lifted me up through all the good and the bad things.

To my industry friends and the amazing publicists from the PR List who answered my posts and emails with your valuable and insightful advice, scenarios, and suggestions.

For all of the artists highlighted and mentioned throughout this book - we don't have anything to publicize without your talent, hard work, and willingness to keep going.

To all of my clients past and present who put your trust in me to represent you and help you through this crazy new music business.

I am so sad that Jay Frank is not here to celebrate the milestone of this book and my agency's 25-year anniversary. He was one of my greatest friends and I still can't believe he's gone.

I also miss my friend and co-author of the Cyber PR Teachers Guide, Rich Meitin, who called me from a rehab center months before he died to tell me all of the reasons he loved me and loved collaborating with me. I am honored I got to collaborate with him.

Index

T

U-V

CPSIA information can be obtained
at www.ICGtesting.com
Printed in the USA
LVHW091939270521
688707LV00009BA/304/J